Old and New Terrorism

To my students

Old and New Terrorism

Late Modernity, Globalization and the
Transformation of Political Violence

PETER R. NEUMANN

polity

First published in 2009 by Polity Press

Polity Press
65 Bridge Street
Cambridge CB2 1UR, UK

Polity Press
350 Main Street
Malden, MA 02148, USA

ISBN-13: 978-0-7456-4375-5
ISBN-13: 978-0-7456-4376-2(PB)

A catalogue record for this book is available from the British Library.

Typeset in 10.25 on 13 pt FF Scala
by Servis Filmsetting Ltd, Stockport, Cheshire
Printed and bound by MPG Books Group, UK

The publisher has used its best endeavours to ensure that the URLs for external websites referred to in this book are correct and active at the time of going to press. However, the publisher has no responsibility for the websites and can make no guarantee that a site will remain live or that the content is or will remain appropriate.

Every effort has been made to trace all copyright holders, but if any have been inadvertently overlooked the publishers will be pleased to include any necessary credits in any subsequent reprint or edition.

For further information on Polity, visit our website: www.politybooks.com.

Contents

CHAPTER ONE

Introduction

Two years before the September 11 attacks against the United States in 2001, the pre-eminent historian of terrorism, Walter Laqueur, noted that a 'revolution' in the character of terrorism was taking place. In his view, the 'new terrorism' was no longer about the vicious yet calculated application of violence that everyone had become familiar with. Instead, the world was confronted with terrorists whose aim was 'to liquidate all satanic forces [and destroy] all life on earth, as the ultimate punishment for mankind's crimes'.[1] There were no longer any limits to the kinds of weapons these people could use in pursuit of their apocalyptic aims. Their arsenal, Laqueur believed, would soon begin to include not just biological, chemical and nuclear devices but weapons which had previously been considered science fiction. Terrorists, he predicted, would set out to construct 'earthquake machines' and launch 'artificial meteors with which to bombard the earth'.[2] The prospects, in other words, were catastrophic. Terrorism had degenerated into a form of irrational bloodlust which could burst out anywhere and for any reason. Indeed, a few years earlier, Laqueur had claimed that the transformation was of such a magnitude that the conventional vocabulary had become inadequate. In his own words, the 'new' terrorism went 'beyond terrorism as we have known it. New definitions and new terms may have to be developed for new realities.'[3]

Though perhaps alone in the belief that terrorists would get hold of 'earthquake machines', Laqueur was not the only expert who sensed that the nature of terrorism was changing.[4] During the 1990s, many of the terrorist groups that had kept researchers busy during the 1970s and 1980s had decided to abandon violence. The Palestinian Liberation Organization (PLO), which had fought Israel in the name of Palestinian nationalism for decades and was responsible for one of the most spectacular terrorist attacks prior to the September 11 attacks – the kidnapping of eleven Israeli athletes during the Olympic Games in Munich in 1972 – recognized Israel and publicly renounced the use of terrorism. The Irish Republican Army (IRA), whose campaign to end the British 'occupation' and create a united Ireland had spanned 25 years and brought Northern Ireland to the brink of civil war, had called a 'permanent' ceasefire, paving the way for inclusion in a peaceful settlement of the conflict. And in April 1998, the German Red Army Faction (RAF), an extreme left-wing group which had threatened the stability of the West German state with its campaign of kidnappings and assassinations in the late 1970s, finally declared its campaign to be over, announcing that 'The urban guerrilla in the shape of the RAF is now history.'[5]

On the other hand, new and more dangerous forms of terrorism seemed to be on the rise. In early 1993, a group of Islamist extremists – led by Ramzi Yousef and inspired by the radical Egyptian cleric Omar Abdel Rahman – launched the first attack on the World Trade Center in New York, hoping to cause mass civilian casualties and bring down one of the towers altogether.[6] Two years later, in March 1995, the Buddhist-inspired cult Aum Shinrikyo – in an attempt to hasten the impending apocalypse – contaminated the Tokyo underground with the nerve gas Sarin, resulting in twelve deaths and more than a thousand injured people.[7] Just one month later, an American right-wing extremist, Timothy McVeigh, set off a large truck bomb in Oklahoma City which killed 168 people – the most deadly act of terrorism committed on American soil prior to the attacks of 11 September 2001.

It seemed obvious that a change of guard was taking place: one by one, the 'usual suspects' were leaving the scene, making way for a new set of terrorists whose violence appeared even more unpredictable and indiscriminate. Like Laqueur, many experts anticipated the increasing use of weapons of mass destruction by terrorists – leading up to the possibility of a 'nuclear Armageddon' – while others tried to outdo each other by inventing ever more dramatic names for the looming threat. The new phenomenon was frequently described as 'super-terrorism' or 'mega-terrorism'; some even talked about 'hyper-terrorism'.[8] Whatever their differences in vocabulary and emphasis, there was no doubt in most minds that the world was confronted with a 'new' type of terrorism – one that was more deadly and dangerous than any other kind of terrorism previously seen.[9]

The trouble was that none of the self-styled experts could provide a coherent explanation for what was happening. As a result, members of the 'terrorism studies' fraternity attempted to extract wide-ranging insights about the causes and possible solutions for violent conflict based on their 'terroristic' manifestations rather than by studying the conflicts from which they arose.[10] Acts of terrorism, in other words, were looked at as if they were free-standing social phenomena with no need for further examination of context and circumstances. In practice, instead of trying to understand the nature of political, social, economic and cultural change and deduce its implications for conflicts in which terrorism has occurred (or may occur), many terrorism researchers merely saw bombs going off in places they had not considered relevant and for reasons which they had not thought of. With the notable exception of the American scholar Bruce Hoffman, who traced some of the key developments with great insight and precision,[11] the concept of 'new terrorism' was frequently used as a slogan which signalled that things were different from how they had been but provided no real explanation of why things had changed. Because they focused on the 'thin crust' of terrorist violence rather than the 'very deep pie' of changes in the global environment[12] which had created different conditions for terrorism to materialize, many terrorism analysts missed out on the underlying causes of what they sought to understand. Unsurprisingly, predictions such as Laqueur's turned out to be deeply flawed.

What this book is about

This book investigates how and why terrorism in recent decades has changed. However, rather than merely looking at the 'thin crust' of terrorism, it will describe and explain the new terrorism as a result of the 'very deep pie' of changes in the global environment and the conditions they have helped to create. Indeed, it argues that much of contemporary terrorism is a unique expression of these conditions and, in particular, that the new terrorism cannot be understood without making sense of the dynamics that have been caused by late modernity and globalization.

First, this book will look at how terrorist groups function as organizations and how globalization has altered their structures and modus operandi. Through the so-called information revolution – principally, of course, the rise of the Internet – terrorist groups can maintain, communicate with and respond to global constituencies. This, and the relative ease with which it has become possible to move from one country to another, has enabled terrorist groups to establish diffuse networks that span continents and allow for an unparalleled degree of flexibility and operational reach. Equally important, globalization has fostered different mindsets and identities that have permitted terrorists to overcome national boundaries and expand into transnational space.

Second, the book will examine the new political agendas of terrorist groups and explain how they have been shaped by the conditions inherent in globalization and late modernity. As often pointed out, late modernity and globalization are dialectic processes that involve both integration and fragmentation: while providing immense benefits for an increasingly cosmopolitan elite, they have triggered the rise of political paradigms that revolve around particularist forms of ethnic and – especially – religious identity, rejecting the universal, secular and liberal norms which late modernity and globalization are meant to promote.[13] As will be shown, it is in this context that the religious revival, the politicization of religion and, ultimately, the rise of religiously inspired terrorism must be understood.

Finally, the book will investigate the changing nature of terrorist violence and demonstrate how late modernity and globalization can explain it. Faced with media saturation and desensitization, terrorists need to engage in ever more vicious forms of violence in order to 'get through' and achieve the psychological effect on which the strategy of terrorism relies. Based on the rise of particularist ideologies which define all members of the ethnic or religious 'other' as 'infidels' or subhuman, there are fewer restraints that would prevent terrorists from employing violence against non-combatants. Taken together, this lack of ideological restraints and the need to 'get through' form a strategic environment in which extreme forms of brutality and mass-casualty attacks against civilians become possible.

Based on this analysis, the book concludes that both governments and societies are ill-prepared to face the challenge of the new terrorism. The institutions charged with fighting terrorism must flatten their hierarchies and tear down the barriers to international cooperation. They also need to begin to take on the new terrorists' message in the kind of (virtual) spaces in which most of their potential supporters now socialize and from which they receive much of their information. Controversially, the book asserts that crude – albeit well-intentioned – attempts to impose hyper-universalist ideologies such as 'cosmopolitanism' risk making the ideological blowback of late modernity and globalization even worse. Instead, the way forward lies in softening the interpretations of religious, ethnic or national identities and in providing avenues through which they can be expressed non-violently.

Key concepts and definitions

Needless to say, none of the propositions put forward in this book are entirely straightforward. It makes sense, therefore, to begin by explaining how key terms and concepts will be understood. In the case of terrorism, for example, there is no agreed definition in international law, nor is there a consensus among scholars.[14] The phenomenon is complex and its meaning has changed over the centuries, ranging from the state 'terror' of the French Revolution to the small, non-state groups which represent a more contemporary understanding of 'terrorism'.[15] The main problem, however, is that the term is politically contested[16] and that – consequently – its descriptive and normative uses are constantly conflated in the public discourse. For some, terrorism describes a particular type of violent activity but implies no opinion or judgement about the righteousness of the act or the cause for which it was committed. For others, it is a word of condemnation reserved for all kinds of actions that are considered illegitimate and morally reprehensible. Hence, whereas for the latter, 'terrorist' and 'freedom fighter' are mutually exclusive, in the eyes of the former, one may well be a terrorist and a freedom fighter at the same time.[17]

There have been numerous diplomatic efforts aimed at producing an agreed definition of terrorism. All these initiatives have, in essence, been about trying to narrow the gap between the descriptive and normative uses of the word. On the one hand, terrorism needed to be turned into an objectively 'definable' activity – something which could not be dismissed as a biased political judgement. On the other hand, the whole point of defining the activity was to facilitate strong measures *against* it, so it still needed to be clear that terrorism, however defined, was a 'bad thing'. The formula which many governments and international organizations have decided to adopt describes terrorism as politically motivated violence that intentionally targets civilians and non-combatants. This definition seems to distinguish terrorism from other forms of violence, yet it also carries a normative statement because violence against 'innocents' is considered a taboo in all cultures. Although there continues to be no full and comprehensive definition of terrorism in international law, the approach has been adopted in various United Nations Security Council Resolutions dealing with terrorism, and it was endorsed by the UN Secretary General in March 2005.[18] In fact, even in scholarly circles, the idea of terrorism as the deliberate use of violence against civilians appears to have gained ground, with various prominent authors using definitions to this effect.[19]

Politically, therefore, a compromise may have been found – but does it actually make sense? Arguably, the consensus definition is too narrow as well as too broad. It is too narrow because it fails to include acts of violence that clearly should be considered terrorism. Take, for instance, the IRA's bombing campaign against the financial district of London in the early 1990s when attacks were launched in the evening and multiple warnings were issued so that office buildings could be evacuated in time. Civilian casualties were not intended, but the IRA wanted to cause terror, inflict heavy financial losses and intimidate the British government into making concessions. If not terrorism, what else did these attacks represent? At the same time, the definition is too broad because it fits all kinds of activities which are not normally regarded as terrorism. The Holocaust, for example, and the Rwandan genocide were both acts of politically motivated violence and they both involved the deliberate killing of innocents but they would not normally be categorized as acts of terrorism.

The definitional problem, which has haunted as well as hindered research on terrorism for many decades, is unlikely to be resolved by this author and/or by this contribution. Strictly for the purposes of this book, then, terrorism – as a method rather than as a social phenomenon – will be thought of as *the deliberate creation of fear, usually through the use (or threat of use) of symbolic acts of violence, to influence the political behaviour of a target group.* This definition draws on the work by T. P. Thornton, whose main study – although over forty years old – still forms one of the most informative and insightful analyses of terrorism. It highlights the violent quality of most terrorist acts, which distinguishes a programme of terror from other forms of non-violent propagation, such as mass demonstrations and boycotts. It also stresses the particular quality of terrorist violence. Thornton referred to it as 'extra-normal'; that is, for a certain level of organized political violence to be called terrorism, it must go beyond the norms of violent political agitation accepted by a given society. Finally, and perhaps most importantly, Thornton's definition emphasizes the symbolic nature of the violent act.[20] An act of terrorist violence will attempt to convey a message to a target audience rather than secure a piece of territory (as in conventional war) or extinguish a people or ethnic group (as in genocide).[21]

The terms globalization and, to a lesser extent, late modernity may score not far behind terrorism in the list of political buzzwords. Late modernity, which is often thought to have

'begun' after the end of the Second World War, describes
the latest phase of modernity in which the social, political
and economic processes that marked the modern era – the
rise of capitalism and representative democracy, urbanization, and industrialization – have reached a new stage. Still
rooted in modernity (hence, 'late' rather than 'post' modernity), prominent sociologists such as Anthony Giddens and
Zygmunt Bauman believe that late modernity represents a
'radicalized' version of modernity in which some of the trends
and processes that were present in modernity continue but
have been accelerated, prompting substantive changes in the
ways we live and work and leading to a seemingly all-pervasive
sense of uncertainty.[22] Globalization, which as an academic
concept caught on in the 1990s, is widely seen as part of
this process and is, in fact, believed to be one of the defining characteristics of late modernity. Giddens, for example,
looks at globalization as an outgrowth of modernity rather
than a separate development. Modernity and late modernity,
he argues, are 'inherently globalizing',[23] and indeed this book
will show that, in many instances, it is difficult to understand
one without the other(s).

What, then, is globalization? Sceptics argue that the international system is no more integrated now than it was in earlier
historical periods, and that globalization is neither novel
nor valid or relevant as a concept to describe change in the
global political system.[24] There can be no question that these
claims merit examination and debate, but it should be obvious that this book will disappoint those who reject the notion
of globalization altogether. The assumption underlying this
book is that globalization exists, that it represents a unique
set of processes which have produced changes in degree and
kind, and that its effects – though uneven – can be felt across
the world. According to the British academics David Held
and Anthony McGrew, globalization describes (and can be

measured in) four kinds of processes: a 'stretching' of activities beyond national borders (extensity); the intensification of such activities (intensity); the 'speeding up' of global interactions (velocity); and, consequently, the growing significance of events and decisions in distant places (impact).[25] Thus defined, globalization can be said to have given rise not just to increased transnational flows of people, goods, capital and information but also to the creation of new 'transcontinental or interregional . . . networks of activity, interaction, and the exercise of power'.[26]

It seems clear that important political events such as the end of the Cold War, as well as developments in communication, information technology and transportation, helped accelerate the deepening and widening of global integration, with many of its most profound consequences becoming obvious in the 1990s. The roots of the phenomenon, however, are more complex and date back further in time. Moreover, although, like modernity, globalization may have been driven to a significant extent by developments in the economic sphere, it would be mistaken to view globalization as purely economic in its causes and consequences. The drivers of globalization can also be found in politics, culture and technology, and its impact has been felt in all these spheres of human activity, extending even to the cognitive – expressed, for example, in people's changing sense of identity and their growing interest in, and realization of, how events in faraway countries affect their lives.[27]

Like terrorism, the term 'globalization' will be used in a purely descriptive manner. Some of the prominent supporters of globalization – sometimes referred to as 'globalists'[28] – have depicted the phenomenon in glowingly positive terms, predicting that it will lead to an end to poverty, a rise in civic activism, international cooperation and cultural harmony. They ignore that many of the developments associated with globalization do not by themselves determine any particular outcome. When the *New York Times* journalist Thomas Friedman talks about 'super-empowered individuals', he may have Bill Gates in mind,[29] yet – arguably – the very same processes have also empowered Osama bin Laden. And when former US President Bill Clinton says that people can do 'more public good than ever before, because of the rise of NGOs [non-governmental organizations], because of the global media culture and because of the Internet',[30] he fails to mention that all these tools of globalization are also being used by extremists in order to spread violence and hatred. In shedding light on the 'darker' side of globalization, this book hopes to correct a partial and (often) naive perspective of globalization and its consequences.

Before delving into the analysis of how late modernity and globalization have facilitated the rise of the new terrorism, it is important to discuss the meaning of the labels 'old' and 'new'. The question of whether new terrorism really deserves the label 'new' has been debated vigorously ever since the concept emerged.[31] In fact, a similar debate followed the publication of Mary Kaldor's book, *New and Old Wars*, which argued that globalization had altered the nature of violent conflict more generally.[32] In both cases, many scholars, particularly historians, felt that the label 'new' was not justified because none of the developments described were unprecedented or unique. While few disputed that anything at all had changed, most of the sceptics maintained that historical precedents could be found for all the trends that had been identified by the proponents of the 'new terrorism' or 'new war' hypotheses, who – so the argument went – had failed to appreciate the 'essential continuities with previous expressions' of organized political violence.[33] Some of these interventions were both timely and accurate, especially in the period immediately following the September 11 attacks, when policy makers in the

United States conveyed the impression that the threat they were dealing with was unprecedented in human history and that nothing could be learned from previous experiences.

However, without wanting to be pedantic, it is important to point out that, linguistically, the adjective 'new' does not depict phenomena that are unprecedented. Rather, it tends to be used in the context of evolutionary change.[34] When the fax machine was invented, it was not talked about as the 'new fax' because there had been no fax machine prior to it being invented. Instead, it was correctly referred to as a 'new' form of electronic communication, drawing on technology used in the telex and other means of communication which had preceded the fax. Likewise, far from ignoring or denying the 'essential historical continuities' in terrorism, the notion of 'new terrorism' stresses the fact that some of the current manifestations of terroristic violence are not unprecedented, but that they need to be understood in the wider context of the evolving character of terrorism. Reflecting on the concept of 'new wars', the academic Thomas Weiss captured the essence of what 'newness' is about: 'It is not so much that totally new elements have appeared as that elements thought extinct or tangential have come to the fore or been combined in ways that were heretofore unremarkable or largely unknown.'[35] Indeed, it is the idea of significant – though by no means sudden or unprecedented – change that the notion of 'new' terrorism hopes to embody.

Another common misunderstanding is the supposition that the transformation towards 'new terrorism' has been uniform and universal. Critics of the concept frequently point to examples of 'old' terrorists whose campaigns seem to have been unaffected by the rise of the 'new terrorism' as evidence that the concept is irrelevant.[36] This, however, does not diminish the concept's validity. None of the proponents of 'new terrorism' has suggested that all terrorist groups have suddenly turned into mass-casualty producing transnational networks.

Some may have gone all the way, while others have partly transformed, picking and choosing from the menu of new options. This reflects the needs and strategies of particular terrorist organizations, and it also mirrors the peculiar ways in which the processes of late modernity and globalization have unfolded. In fact, the consequences of 'new terrorism' are best understood not as a question of either/or ('new' versus 'old') but, rather, in terms of degree ('new*er*' versus 'old*er*'). As this book will demonstrate, even those terrorists who have stubbornly refused to adapt to the new imperatives and possibilities have, in one way or another, been affected by the 'new terrorism'.

Needless to say, all these claims will be substantiated and illustrated in the main part of this book. Chapter 2 will derive 'ideal types' of old and new terrorism and illustrate their key features with two case studies. Chapters 3 to 5 explore the causes of the transformation from old to new: chapter 3 looks at how globalization has changed terrorist groups as organizations; chapter 4 examines how the conditions inherent in late modernity and globalization have facilitated the rise of religiously inspired terrorism; and chapter 5 aims to understand the causes of the changing nature of terrorist violence, drawing on the themes that were developed in earlier chapters.

It should be obvious that the transformation that could be witnessed in recent years has significant implications for the way in which terrorism should be countered. It raises profound questions about the manner in which governmental institutions charged with fighting terrorism are organized, but also about the kinds of political, ideological and societal responses that are necessary to tackle it. Hence, although this book is not primarily about counter-terrorism, chapter 6 – the conclusion – will spell out many of these questions, suggest some possible answers and provide some informed speculation about the future of terrorism.

CHAPTER TWO

Old and New Terrorism

One of the most interesting debates about the nature of the new terrorism took place in the pages of the journal *Survival* little more than a year prior to the September 11 attacks against the United States.[1] Daniel Benjamin and Steven Simon, two former officials at the National Security Council in the United States, argued that the new terrorism was about the use of weapons of mass destruction and that Osama bin Laden was its key protagonist. Bruce Hoffman, then a Director at the RAND Corporation, disagreed. He asserted that, even though the rise in religiously inspired terrorism formed part of the new terrorism, it was mistaken to focus on one individual at the expense of the global network of which he was part. Hoffman also questioned the widespread 'obsession' with weapons of mass destruction, when all the evidence showed that terrorists had always been, and were likely to remain, operationally conservative.[2]

The dispute illustrated how even people with similar assumptions and backgrounds, who shared the idea that a new kind of terrorism had emerged, still had very different ideas of what it was. Indeed, during the late 1990s, the notion of new terrorism became a catch-all for everything that seemed novel or unusual, and the resulting debates between supporters and opponents often ended in widespread confusion because there existed no shared understanding of the concept and its key characteristics. For this book, it will be essential, therefore, to go back to first principles and distil the 'essence' of the new terrorism before attempting to explain how it came about.

As a method of describing the transformation from 'old' to 'new' terrorism, the changes that have occurred will be captured in three variables which, taken together, define terrorism as a social phenomenon.[3] The first of these variables refers to the *structures* in which terrorists are organized. Terrorist groups may differ in size but – with nearly no exception – they are always smaller than their adversaries. In fact, it is the notion of being pitted against a stronger and seemingly all-powerful enemy that often determines their perception of the struggle in which they are engaged. Moreover, while there may be terrorists who are able to act more openly than others (for example, those who are provided safe haven by a state sponsor or when operating in a 'weak' or 'failing' state), even in the most trouble-free environment, there remains an element of conspiracy which will be reflected in their respective modus operandi.[4]

All this, of course, can be said for a whole range of entities including, for instance, groups engaged in organized crime, which are also relatively small (compared to the law enforcement agencies that are trying to thwart their activities) and forced to operate in secret. Clearly, what makes terrorist groups different from criminal networks are the *aims* of their activity. Whether we approve of their ideas or not, terrorist groups are political organizations whose principal objective is not financial gain but the transformation of a social and political order. The ideologies that underpin their campaigns may be vastly different in nature – Marxist, fascist, nationalist, or religious, to name but the most popular – but what all terrorists share is a desire for their respective view of the world to become the paradigm according to which societies ought to be run.

Finally, it is also the *method* of achieving political change by which terrorism can be distinguished from other social phenomena. Terrorists hope to achieve political change through violence, and they believe that it will be possible to do so by relying, to a significant extent, on symbolic acts of extra-normal violence whose purpose is the creation of fear (see chapter 1). The choice of this particular method may be influenced by terrorists' perception of relative weakness and the consequent belief that spectacular acts of violence are necessary in order to 'get through' to their audience. Equally, it may be inspired by the hope that such violence will provoke repression and lead to a loss of legitimacy for those in power; or by the belief that acts of terrorism will mobilize and trigger an uprising of the masses.[5] Whatever their strategy, terrorists have convinced themselves that it is this particular method – used, sometimes, in conjunction with others – that offers the best chance of turning their aspirations into reality.

As a social phenomenon, then, terrorism consists of small conspiracies (structure) aiming to achieve political objectives (aim) through symbolic acts of extra-normal violence (method). Thus understood, it becomes easier not only to distinguish terrorism from other forms of organized violence but also to conceptualize the changes that have occurred within terrorism.

Indeed, 'structure', 'aim' and 'method' are the three categories and/or variables that will be used in the following to construct 'ideal types' of old and new terrorism and identify the key trends whose origins will be explained in the following chapters.

In the first section, it will be shown how terrorist groups have changed their structures from hierarchy to network, sometimes with transnational reach; that religion has come to be a prominent source of their aims and ideologies; and how their methods have shifted towards the application of more excessive and indiscriminate forms of violence. In the second and third section of this chapter, these trends – which, taken together, constitute the new terrorism – will be illustrated by examining two case studies, the IRA and Al Qaeda.

Comparing old and new terrorism

The critics of the new terrorism argue that historical precedents can be found for all the developments that have been
identified as new and that, therefore, the concept as a whole is
flawed.[6] As will be shown in this section, the reality is rather
more complex. The transformation from old to new has often
been gradual, and – rather than completely reinventing the
idea of terrorism – the new terrorism naturally draws on
themes and ideas which have existed in earlier periods.

Structures

The first area in which change has taken place is that of terrorist group *structures*. All terrorist groups, new and old, have
always portrayed themselves as regular armies, engaged in
legitimate struggles and representing real authority. Yet, prior
to the emergence of new terrorism, terrorist groups not only
mimicked traditional armies' rhetoric and insignia but also
their structures. Initially, many groups adopted hierarchical
systems with clear lines of command and control, sometimes
even assigning military ranks. After suffering their first losses,
they often realized that conventional military-type structures
were too transparent, too easy to disrupt and, therefore, completely unsuitable for organizations which had to operate in
secret. As a result, many adopted the supposedly more flexible
cell system. Cells typically consisted of up to a dozen members,
with only the cell leader having any contact or relations with the
wider organization, so that – when individual members were
caught – they could only betray the other members of their cell
rather than implicating the entire organization. Any potential
damage from arrests or informers would thus be limited.[7]

The cell system has mistakenly been described as being
'independent of hierarchical control' and having 'no central
organization'.[8] In reality, the key attraction and advantage

of the cell system lies in the fact that it *preserves* the group's hierarchy, except for making it less visible to outsiders and the foot soldiers at its bottom. Through the cell leader, individual cells are fully integrated into the chain of command. They are only autonomous to the extent to which the leadership has explicitly granted them autonomy. Indeed, in most of the terrorist groups that have been organized in cells, it would have been inconceivable for individual cells to embark on major operations without seeking prior approval from the group's leadership. The adoption of a cell system does not, therefore, represent a qualitative shift: cells are as old as terrorism, and they are not what is meant when referring to the diffusion of terrorist group structures.

Another feature of old terrorist groups is for their structures to revolve around one physical centre of gravity. It is this geographical focal point – be it a country, part of a country, or a territory straddling several countries – from which the terrorist group draws most of its recruits, where the bulk of its operations are carried out and against whose government or authorities its campaign is directed. This, of course, does not exclude the possibility of international linkages. There exists a long tradition of mobilizing diaspora communities to support the struggle 'back home',[9] and it seems obvious that even old terrorists have frequently gone abroad in order to collaborate with others, receive training from state sponsors, prepare attacks, or strike at targets associated with their adversary. Yet, regardless of how extensive such activities were, they were always geared towards supporting the central theatre of operations. In other words, their purpose was to sustain and strengthen rather than shift the centre of gravity.

This was obviously true for many of the old ethno-nationalist groups whose struggle focused on one particular territory. But it also applied to the adherents of supposedly global ideologies, such as the Marxist terrorists in Western Europe in the 1970s and 1980s who mostly had just one centre of gravity towards which their activities and operations were directed. The German Red Army Faction, for instance, may have espoused world revolution, and it regularly associated – and often collaborated – with ideological brethren from across the globe. But its aim and priority was to topple the (West) German government, its recruits were all German, and its active operational structures were all firmly based in Germany.[10] Despite all the internationalist rhetoric, the old Marxist terrorists, like all other old terrorists, gravitated around the places from which they had come.

By contrast, the structures of the new terrorism are more diffuse. They are often described as networks rather than as organizations because formalized hierarchies have been replaced with personal relationships. What matters is not someone's formal rank but whom they know and what connections they can facilitate. John Arquilla and David Ronfeldt, two American analysts who coined the idea of 'netwar', described the new kind of network as follows: 'There is no single central leader or commander; the network as a whole . . . has little to no hierarchy,' appearing 'both acephalous (headless) and polycephalous (Hydra-headed)' at the same time.[11] Within networked structures, individuals with numerous links to other members of the network emerge as 'hubs', but there can be many 'hubs' and 'middle managers' within a network, so that the elimination of individual hubs may do little damage to the network as a whole. Accordingly, Arquilla and Ronfeldt concluded that networks are not only flat but also quite robust.[12]

New terrorist networks often have no firm rules on how operations are initiated and authorized. The decision to carry out an operation can lie with groups of affiliated nodes who may (or may not) choose to consult more senior members of the network. In most networks, there exists a nominal leadership that provides inspiration, justification and guidance, and is in some way connected to the wider movement. Others, however, may operate as a form of 'leaderless resistance' in which there is no operational connection at all among individual 'cells' as well as between the 'cells' and those who provide ideological guidance and inspiration.[13] According to Louis Beam, the American right-wing theorist who first articulated the idea: 'No one need issue an order to anyone. Those idealist[s] truly committed to the cause of freedom will act when they feel the time is ripe or will take their cue from others who precede them.'[14]

Another novelty lies in how terrorist organizations have become increasingly transnational in reach and orientation. In contrast to international movements, transnational terrorist movements not only reach across borders but create an entirely new kind of social space which has no single, permanent geographical point of reference and is beyond the control of a single state.[15] Based on the association with this (often virtual) space, members of such networks develop strong identifications that supersede any identity related to the location in which they are (physically) based.[16] Consequently, transnational terrorist networks may recruit their members from across the world rather than any one country in particular. Moreover, while there may be one geographical centre of gravity at any given point in time, this point can shift depending on changing ideological emphases or the group's assessment of where victory is most likely. In fact, the place in which most of the group's operations take place may not be identical to the place from which the majority of its recruits originate or where its leadership is based.

Critics of the concept have invoked a small number of historical instances of transnational mobilization as evidence that there is nothing new about the phenomenon.[17] The most frequently cited example is the early Anarchist movement, which emerged in the late nineteenth century and operated in – and received support from across – Europe and North America. The exploits of the Russian group Narodnaya Volya, which killed Tsar Alexander II in 1878, inspired a string of assassinations and bombings in Spain, England, France, Germany and, most dramatically, the United States, where a young Hungarian-born immigrant killed President William McKinley.[18] When taking a closer look at the historical research, however, it quickly becomes obvious that the movement largely consisted of a series of national campaigns with only a small amount of cross-border activity or exchange.[19] Activists were linked by a shared ideology, but they mostly fought separate campaigns, which makes the Anarchist movement more similar to the Marxist terrorists of the 1970s and 1980s than Al Qaeda in the 1990s and 2000s.

Even if the example had been accurate, this would not necessarily have proved that the rise of transnational activism is an old phenomenon. In fact, social movement theorists will not find it difficult to identify many other instances of early transnational activism – violent and non-violent – beginning with the Republican movement in Europe in the late eighteenth century. There can be no doubt, therefore, that historical continuities exist. At the same time, all the experts agree that, compared to earlier historical periods, recent decades have seen a steep increase. Sidney Tarrow, one of the world's leading experts and author of a book with the title *The New Transnational Activism*, asserts that 'There is more of it . . . it involves a broader spectrum of ordinary people and elites, and . . . it extends to a wider range of domestic and international concerns.'[20] If this is true for social movements generally, why should terrorism be any different?

Aims

Significant change can also be found when looking at the second variable, the terrorists' *aims and ideologies*. The ideologies of terrorist groups are often mistakenly thought of as existing in a space completely separate from the (non-violent) political mainstream. In reality, terrorists' political ideas always tend to reflect a given society's radical ideological currents, with the obvious difference that terrorists are pursuing those (radical) ends through violent means. Indeed, in the early 1990s, Leonard Weinberg showed that the majority of terrorist groups have emerged as splinters of political parties, which proves that – ideologically – terrorism, terrorist groups and their activists are often rooted in conventional political activism and discourses.[21]

It should come as no surprise, then, that in earlier decades, when most of the radical social and political movements were either Marxist or nationalist, these ideologies were also dominant among the terrorist groups of the time. The desire for national self-determination was among the most significant political forces that shaped twentieth-century history. It produced countless 'national liberation movements', of which many used guerrilla warfare or terrorism in their pursuit of independence. This was true for many territories which had formed part of one of the European empires, but it also found its expression in the peripheral regions of established European states, where minorities reasserted their (often long-forgotten) national and ethnic identities.[22]

In the second half of the twentieth century, Marxism came to represent an equally powerful discourse which attracted large numbers – especially among the first post-war generation in western countries and in Latin America – into radical political movements. As with nationalism, numerous terrorist groups emerged as the violent outgrowths of larger political movements. Indeed, during the 1960s, 1970s and 1980s, many terrorist groups embraced both Marxism and nationalism at the same time. The vast ideological differences between (particularist) nationalism and (internationalist) Marxism could be glossed over with reference to the idea of 'anti-impe-rialism', which appeared to reconcile the struggle for national self-determination with the fight against 'neo-colonialism'.[23]

In the 1980s and 1990s, religious issues gradually found their way back into the mainstream political discourse. Whereas in the 1960s and 1970s traditional religious move-ments across the world struggled to find supporters – never mind having any political influence – the subsequent decades saw a revival of religion and religiously inspired political move-ments which few observers would have predicted. This could be seen in the United States, where the evangelical movement organized itself into a formidable political force that helped pave the way for Ronald Reagan's presidency and was instru-mental in the election and re-election of George W. Bush.[24] It was also evident in India, where Hindu nationalism asserted itself against the more inclusive notions of Indian autonomy and self-rule embodied by the Congress Party. Its Hindu nationalist counterpart, the Indian People's Party (BJP), was established in 1980 and came to power in 1996. Not least, of course, the rise of religiously inspired political movements could be witnessed in the Muslim world: Ayatollah Khomeini took power in Iran in 1979; in Arab countries like Egypt and Syria, the Muslim Brothers managed to sideline their secular rivals as the only serious challengers to authoritarian rule;[25] and in Afghanistan, the Soviet occupation attracted Muslim volunteers from all over the world willing to fight (and die) under the banner of jihad.

The Swedish academic Magnus Ranstorp was among the first to note that 'Almost all the contemporary terrorist groups with a religious imperative are either offshoots or on the fringe of broader movements.'[26] And indeed, as with Marxism and nationalism, the emergence of radical religiously inspired political movements came to be reflected in a number of religiously oriented terrorist groups. Hoffman shows that, whereas in the late 1960s not a single terrorist group any-where in the world could be described as religiously inspired, the share of religiously motivated groups had risen to nearly a third by the mid-1990s.[27] This included militant Christian anti-abortionists in the United States, Jewish extremists in the West Bank, the Buddhist-inspired cult Aum Shinrikyo (responsible for the nerve gas attack on the Tokyo under-ground in 1995) and various groups in the Muslim world ranging from Hezbollah and Hamas to Al Qaeda. Though with some qualifications, even critical commentators have come to accept that, at the international level, 'religious extremism has . . . become the most powerful motivational and ideological basis for groups engaged in terrorist activity.'[28]

Other ideological drivers have not disappeared, of course, and analysts such as Ekaterina Stepanova are right to point to the continued strength of radical nationalism at the domestic level.[29] It is equally important, however, to note that, in many of the places where the type of nationalism adopted by terror-ist groups used to be secular and left-wing, it is now mixed with religious themes. Nowhere is this more obvious than in the Palestinian territories, where the fight for 'national libera-tion' had been initiated and led by the Palestinian Liberation Organization (PLO), which was dominated by Yasser Arafat's non-religious Fatah movement and various Marxist groups. Unchallenged for more than two decades, the late 1980s saw the rise of Hamas – an offspring of the Egyptian Muslim Brothers – which first challenged and then overtook Fatah in size and popular support with a vision of national liberation based on a strong religious imperative.[30]

Similar shifts occurred in Chechnya and Kashmir, where long-established secular groups were either transformed or replaced by religiously motivated rivals. In contemporary Iraq, it has become virtually impossible to disentangle the religious and nationalist components of the indigenous insurgent movement.[31] Arguably, then, if nationalism and Marxism used to go hand in glove during the era of old terrorism, the same now seems to apply to nationalism and religion. In most of the cases mentioned above, it makes little sense to establish artificial boundaries between 'religious' on the one and 'nationalist' or 'ethnic' on the other hand. Though not always in equal proportions, they are both.

Method

The third area in which change has occurred is that of terrorism as a *method*. 'Terroristic' violence, of course, is not fundamentally different from what it used to be. As mentioned above, terrorists are 'operationally conservative':[32] 95 per cent of terrorist attacks consist of just a handful of tactics, in particular assassination, bombing, kidnapping and hijacking. Brian Jenkins, one of the longest serving and most highly regarded terrorism analysts, agrees: 'Terrorists blow up things, kill people, or seize hostages. Every terrorist incident is merely a variation on these three activities.'[33] What has changed, then, is not so much the type of operation carried out by terrorist groups but, rather, how they are conducted and against whom.

Needless to say, even old terrorists often killed civilians, and – occasionally – their operations were aimed at producing large numbers of casualties. As Hoffman points out, several precedents for near-simultaneous, mass-casualty attacks, some involving aircraft, can be found as early as the 1980s.[34] It would be mistaken, therefore, to believe that the old terrorists were all knights in shining armour for whom the notion of inflicting pain and suffering on civilian populations would have been intolerable. Even so, Jenkins's well-known assertion that terrorists wanted 'a lot of people watching, not a lot of people dead'[35] was more or less true: killing people was secondary to the communicative effects that could be achieved through a particular act of violence. In the era of the new terrorism, the two considerations – violence and symbolic value – seem to have merged, with mass-casualty attacks against civilian populations being routine and intentional rather than 'mistakes' or 'exceptions' to be blamed on splinter groups or renegade elements.

There are plenty of statistics that bear out the rise of mass-casualty terrorism in no uncertain terms.[36] All such data, however, must be treated with great caution. Different analysts draw on vastly different sets of source data, with some – such as the RAND Chronology of International Terrorism, the so-called ITERATE database, or the US State Department's *Patterns of Global Terrorism* – excluding 'domestic terrorism' in favour of counting incidents of 'international terrorism'. International terrorism, on the other hand, can mean entirely different things depending on one's point of view.[37] To make matters even more complicated, 'genuine' acts of 'international terrorism', however defined, are relatively rare, which means that a very small number of such events can alter, change or create a trend. The American academic David Tucker, for instance, showed that, by removing from the State Department's statistics just three incidents in the second half of the 1990s, the picture that emerged was that of a 'steady increase [of mass-casualty terrorism] over the last 30 years rather than a spectacular surge'.[38] With few incidents to draw on, a small number of 'misattributions' can turn out to be highly significant, especially when considering that casualty numbers do not always accurately reflect the terrorists' intentions.[39] While it would be mistaken, therefore, to rely on quantitative evidence alone, it should be pointed out that there exist no data that show a stagnation or decline in mass-casualty attacks over the past decades. Analysts may argue about exactly how steep the rise has been, but there appears to be a consensus that, however one manipulates the source data, the trend towards more mass-casualty attacks is consistent and well supported.

Even less quantifiable than the rise in the numbers of people killed is the trend towards greater brutality. Partly, this trend is reflected in the deliberate targeting of civilian populations, which – as mentioned above – used to be the exception but has now become intentional and routine. Old terrorists often went to great lengths to justify and legitimate attacks against people who were not members of the security apparatus or in some other way associated with the enemy government. By contrast, some of the new terrorists clearly have no hesitation in making whole populations legitimate targets based on their ethnicity, religious affiliation, or the policies carried out by their governments.

The increase in brutality also becomes evident when look-ing at how individual operations are carried out. The French academic Olivier Roy draws an interesting parallel between the kidnapping and execution of the former Italian prime minister Aldo Moro by the Red Brigades in 1978 and the kidnappings carried out by Al Qaeda in Iraq, which he argues were 'staged in exactly the same way'.[40] What Roy fails to recognize is that – although both groups used video record-ings in order to communicate their demands – Al Qaeda in Iraq killed its victims in the most grotesquely violent manner (that is, by beheading them), filmed the acts and made the executions publicly available through the Internet. Its central concern was to showcase the violence and brutality of which it was capable, whereas the Red Brigades simply wanted to exploit the sense of drama and public attention which derived from the kidnapping of a high-profile politician.

Arguably, the phenomenon in which the trends towards greater brutality and lethality have merged is terrorists' renewed interest in acquiring and using chemical, biologi-cal, radiological and nuclear materials (CBRN). There are wildly differing estimates regarding the likelihood of attacks involving such materials – ranging from 'imminent' to 'nearly inconceivable'[41] – and it is not the purpose of this book to add another. What seems to be beyond question is that some of the new terrorists have seriously contemplated their use, and that efforts have been undertaken to put such ideas into practice. There continue to be huge difficulties regarding the acquisition and/or production of CBRN materials as well as their dissemination. Indeed, many of those who have tried may well have concluded that the problems are insurmountable and that conventional tactics are more likely to result in successful operations. Even so, it seems clear that ethical and moral constraints against the use of CBRN, though perhaps not entirely absent, are less relevant now than they used to be. Whereas twenty or thirty years ago, none of the major terrorist groups would have considered their use even if they had access to them,[42] many of the new terrorists would seem to have no hesitation in including them in their arsenal if they could be made to work.

One may conclude, therefore, that significant changes have taken place in three areas: the diffusion and transnationalization of terrorist group structures; the rise of religiously inspired ideologies; and the greater lethality and brutality of terrorist operations (see Figure 2.1). To further illustrate these ideas, the rest of this chapter will examine two terrorist groups – the Irish Republican Army and Al Qaeda – which, though by no means perfect examples, bring out some of the key elements of old and new terrorism respectively.

Old terrorism: The Irish Republican Army

For many decades, no study of terrorism would have been complete without an in-depth examination of the Northern Ireland conflict and, in particular, the Provisional Irish

Figure 2.1 Old and new terrorism: 'ideal types'		
	Old terrorism	New terrorism
Structure	Hierarchical; geared towards one centre of gravity	Networked; transnational reach and orientation
Aims	Nationalist and/or Marxist	Religiously inspired
Method	'Legitimate targets'; rules of engagement	Mass-casualty attacks against civilians; excessive violence

Republican Army (IRA). The group came into existence in late 1969, when the long-standing conflict between the pro-British Unionist and pro-Irish Nationalist populations of Northern Ireland had just reignited. The IRA saw itself as the armed vanguard of a united Irish Republic that would include the six counties of Northern Ireland which have always been part of the United Kingdom. In 1994 and 1997, the IRA declared 'permanent ceasefires' which allowed its political wing, Sinn Fein, to become part of the Northern Ireland peace process. In the decade following the conclusion of the Belfast Agreement in 1998, it ceased all operations, decommissioned its arsenal, and – eventually – stood down altogether. Some of its former members are now Sinn Fein ministers in the Northern Ireland power-sharing executive.

IRA structures

Looking at the first variable – structure and organization – it seems clear that the IRA has gone through several mutations. Initially, the group was set up along military lines, with brigades and battalions covering every part of the province. For the IRA leaders at the time, this was the most obvious way in which a 'liberation army' should be organized. It soon became obvious, however, that these structures, which corresponded to local neighbourhoods, were totally unsuitable for the kind of conflict in which the IRA was engaged. By the mid-1970s, when the British government had finally managed to put in place a longer-term political and security strategy for dealing with the conflict, IRA members were being caught by the dozen. An internal IRA report, which was circulated among the leadership in 1976, came to the following conclusions:

> The three-day and seven-day detention orders are breaking volunteers . . . Coupled with this factor, which is contributing to our defeat, we are burdened with an inefficient infra-structure of commands, brigades, battalions and companies. This system with which the Brits and [police Special] Branch are familiar has to be changed. We recommend reorganization and remotivation, the building of a new Irish Republican Army.[43]

This internal reform, which was meant to prepare the IRA for a 'Long War', involved the reorganization of IRA units in line with a cell system. Cells would have four or five members and operate outside their 'home base' as much as possible. Secrecy was paramount, with cell members instructed not to discuss their involvement in the 'armed struggle' with anyone, not even well-known Republicans and members of their families. Relations with the outside world would be maintained by the cell leader.[44] The transformation never quite succeeded to the extent to which it had been envisaged. Some of the rural units resisted the cell structures, arguing that it was hindering communication and that excessive secrecy undermined volunteers' social standing and morale.[45] Still, by the late 1980s, much of the IRA, including some of its most successful units, was operating in line with the new system.

It is important to note that the adoption of the cell system did not foresee any changes to the chain of command. On the contrary, the IRA leadership decreed that cells should have no control over weapons or explosives but that these would be supplied by regional commands when needed for operations.[46] In doing so, the leadership ensured that precious resources were used efficiently, but also – and more importantly – that no operations could be launched without their knowledge.

It remains true, of course, that certain parts of the organization enjoyed more autonomy than others. This became apparent in the 1980s when the movement's leadership under Gerry Adams had adopted its infamous electoral strategy of taking power 'with the Armalite in one hand and the ballot in the other'.[47] As a result, the leadership attempted to make the campaign more 'voter-friendly' by refraining from potentially controversial attacks in the lead-up to important elections. While this resulted in a substantial drop in military activities in the urban areas in which Adams and his 'clique' held sway (in particular Belfast and Derry City), some of the rural units carried on with business as usual.[48]

It would be mistaken, however, to interpret this as a breakdown of the military hierarchy. The leadership, consisting of the seven members of the IRA Army Council, was itself split over the course advocated by Adams so that, arguably, the different policies followed by the different parts of the organization more or less reflected the divisions at the top. Most experts agree that the Army Council – however divided – always remained the supreme decision-making body, and that no major operations or change in strategy would have occurred without its knowledge or approval.[49] In that sense, though sometimes messy, the military hierarchy remained intact.

It is also clear that the IRA's campaign never changed its organizational centre of gravity. The group's sole focus was to end what it saw as the illegal occupation of Northern Ireland by the British government, and its military and other resources were used exclusively in order to achieve this end. The vast majority of IRA operations took place in Northern Ireland. When the group ventured outside the province, it was mainly to attack targets in England, where the aim was to coerce the (British) population into supporting a withdrawal from Northern

Ireland.[50] A few operations took place in Western Europe (especially West Germany, Belgium and the Netherlands) but they were all directed against British military installations.

Needless to say, there existed numerous international linkages. Some of these links had sprung from genuine ideological affinity for other 'liberation movements', such as the close relationship with the Basque Homeland and Liberty (ETA). Others were more instrumental. When it came to fundraising, for instance, the IRA managed to assemble a colourful group of supporters which included, among others, right-wing Irish-Americans, Colonel Gaddafi of Libya, and the Colombian Revolutionary Armed Forces (FARC).[51] Still, no matter how extensive its international linkages, the IRA never adopted another group's agenda as their own nor did IRA members volunteer to become part of foreign struggles. In the IRA's mind, the rationale underlying all international activities was to support the struggle at home rather than any desire or inclination to 'go transnational'.

IRA aims

Considering the IRA's aims and ideology, the group's basic position has been consistent throughout the conflict. It saw itself as a nationalist organization whose aim was to establish an Irish Republic in line with the principles declared by Patrick Pearse and his associates during the Easter Rising of 1916, that is, a 'united Ireland, free and Gaelic'.[52] In the eyes of Irish Republicans, the cause of Ireland's division was not the existence of two antagonistic communities with mutually exclusive national aspirations but the malign influence of the British government who – for various strategic, political and economic reasons – sought to prevent the Irish from realizing their right to self-determination. It was not a conflict, therefore, among the populations of the island but rather one between Irish Republicans and the British state.

From the IRA's viewpoint, even those 26 counties which formed the Irish Free State (today's Republic of Ireland) could not be considered fully free until the remaining six counties in the North had been liberated from British control and 'subjugation'. For the IRA, Britain's presence on the island of Ireland was akin to that of a robber, who '[having broken into your home] . . . tells you, "Get on with your own business, I am only occupying one room"'.[53] In fact, the IRA believed that its aim of achieving freedom and expelling the British occupier could only be achieved through armed force, and that it was the IRA's unique and historic mission to pursue this 'armed struggle'. In Adams's words: 'There are those who tell us that the British Government will not be moved by armed struggle . . . [Yet] the history of Ireland and of colonial involvement throughout the world tells us that they will not be moved by anything else'.[54]

One popular mistake – committed even by some otherwise highly regarded scholars[55] – is for the Northern Ireland conflict to be perceived as a religious conflict because nearly all pro-Irish Nationalists are Catholic, whereas the vast majority of the pro-British Unionists are Protestant. In reality, the principal dimension of the conflict has always been political. The IRA in particular was a secular organization whose members have, on many occasions, derided the influence of the Catholic church over the Nationalist community in Northern Ireland. (The Catholic hierarchy, in turn, has frequently denounced the IRA.)[56] The group has never sought to establish a theocracy or any form of religious government in Ireland but, rather, embraced the notion of a united Republic that would give equal recognition and rights to 'Catholic, Protestant, and Dissenter'. There is not one IRA statement that would cite the Bible or Catholic doctrine in support of, or as justification for, any of its actions. Instead, the group often quotes from the writings of prominent Irish Protestants, such as the leaders of the United Irishmen movement in the late eighteenth century, as a way of highlighting its cross-sectarian nature.[57]

Needless to say, there have always been tensions between the IRA's all-inclusive ideological imperative and rhetoric, and its de facto role as defenders of the Nationalist/Catholic community in Northern Ireland from which it derived much of its popular support. Even so, whenever Irish Republicans clashed with the Unionist community, these conflicts were never related to the Protestants' religious beliefs but were always about their British national and cultural identity, claims and political aspirations.

A stronger ideological inspiration for Irish Republicans than religion was traditional Marxist thought. Since the late nineteenth century, Irish Republican ideology has been influenced by the idea that, because the British colonization of Ireland had – at least partly – been motivated by economic reasons, the new Ireland to be created in the wake of a Republican victory needed to adopt a fundamentally different economic system. Put simply, Irish Republicans believed that the national revolution had to be 'simultaneously a social revolution'.[58] Throughout the IRA's campaign, the declared aim was to create not just a united Ireland but a united *socialist* Ireland. Indeed, IRA leaders regarded the government in Dublin as little more than a neo-colonial puppet whose strings were held by British corporations which continued to exploit the country and prevent the Irish people – even those now living outside the British government's direct influence – from determining their fate freely.

Ultimately, of course, the Marxist agenda remained less important than the group's nationalist aims. After all, the Provisional IRA had emerged as a splinter from the (then) Official IRA, precisely because the Provisionals felt that the Officials' leaders had become 'communists' and were neglecting the defence of the Nationalist community. Martin

McGuinness, now Northern Ireland's Deputy First Minister, initially joined the Officials but quickly switched sides, realizing that the Officials offered hours of political indoctrination but little of the 'action' that he craved.[59] Nevertheless, most Irish Republican activists will happily describe themselves as socialists and anti-imperialists, and the commitment to creating a new economic system has always formed part of what most understood to be the essence of Irish Republicanism.

IRA methods

As far as the nature of the IRA's terrorism is concerned, the statistics make it obvious that the IRA was a very violent organization. It was responsible for more than 1,700 killings in the years 1969–2001 which amounts to nearly half of all conflict-related deaths in that period.[60] The number of 'mass-casualty attacks' carried out by the IRA, however, is relatively small. According to the records available from the Conflict Archive on the Internet at the University of Ulster,[61] there were just seven incidents in which the IRA killed ten or more people: the shooting dead of ten Protestant workers near Kingsmill in January 1976;[62] the killing of ten military bandsmen at Deal in Kent in September 1989; the Remembrance Day bomb in Enniskillen in November 1987, which killed eleven; the killing of eleven soldiers at a military ceremony in Hyde Park in London in 1982; the attack against the La Mon restaurant in County Down in January 1978, which killed twelve; the killing of eighteen British soldiers at Warrenpoint in August 1979; and the Birmingham pub bombings in November 1974, which killed twenty-one.

Of these, only five were planned as mass-casualty incidents: the bombings in Kent, Hyde Park and Warrenpoint were immediately claimed and celebrated as great victories, whereas the Enniskillen and Kingsmill attacks resulted from sectarian tendencies which – though inherent in the

IRA's outlook and approach – were a source of embarrassment and shame for many of the group's more enlightened supporters. The La Mon and Birmingham bombings, on the other hand, were operations gone wrong. In both cases, the intention was to phone in warnings to the police so the premises could be evacuated in time, but the public phones which had been identified were out of action on the day of the operation.[63] This makes the IRA no less responsible for the tragic loss of innocent lives, but it puts into perspective the (quite limited) extent to which the IRA engaged in acts of mass-casualty terrorism.

The difference in reaction to some of the events described above shows that, from the IRA's point of view, not all targets were the same. Uniformed British soldiers and policemen were the most desired because killing them was fully consistent with the IRA's idea of being engaged in a war of national liberation. The same logic applied to other British government representatives and/or symbols of the 'establishment', such as pro-Union politicians, civil servants, ambassadors and even the British royal family. More problematic was the targeting of retired and off-duty security personnel, as well as civilian contractors working for the security services. Though widely seen as legitimate and effective within the IRA, it often led to unease within the wider Nationalist community and prompted accusations of sectarianism and ethnic cleansing from Unionists.[64] Almost inevitably, the IRA also caused a very considerable degree of 'collateral damage', that is, entirely innocent civilians who – though not specifically targeted – got caught up in operations, especially the group's flawed campaign against 'economic targets' (including hotels, shopping centres, restaurants, etc.) that resulted in numerous operational mistakes.

Throughout the 1980s, 25–40 per cent of all IRA victims were civilians, with off-duty personnel representing another

20 per cent. In the three years leading up to the 1994 ceasefire, when the sectarian conflict escalated, the share of civilians killed by the IRA increased sharply, rising to nearly 60 per cent.[65] Even in the last decade of its campaign, therefore, the IRA was not the 'clean killing machine' that it would like to see itself as. Still, there clearly was a rationale whereby targets were selected and legitimacy was sought: IRA violence was meant to be unpredictable, but it was very rarely random. No-warning bombs in crowded places were never considered because engaging in such operations would have been 'dangerous to the image of an Irish liberation movement'.[66] Likewise, while 'enormous amounts of effort' were spent on acquiring ground-to-air missiles to shoot down British army helicopters, the IRA's 'official historian', J. Bowyer Bell, makes it clear that 'literally no serious thought [was given] to biological warfare, gas or poison, much less radiation'.[67]

Furthermore, it should be noted that – in its campaign against the British 'occupation' – acts of excessive violence were quite rare. The IRA wanted to be seen as a national liberation army engaged in a legitimate conflict with the British government, and it was keen, therefore, to distance itself from the activities of the Protestant paramilitary groups who had a long history of extremely violent and sadistic sectarian killings (see chapter 5). In fact, the IRA was at its most vicious when dealing with its own community. The internal policing carried out by the IRA in Republican areas included symbolically harsh punishments, such as the 'knee-capping' of thieves and the 'tarring and feathering' of girls who had 'fraternized' with British soldiers. The dead bodies of IRA members who were suspected of being police informers were dumped alongside busy roads as a warning to others.[68] In the campaign against the British, on the other hand, such cruelty was seen as counterproductive, and – where it occurred – the leadership blamed it on renegades who were said to have acted without proper authority. Even if an entirely 'clean' campaign could never be achieved, the IRA's approach and its intentions were fundamentally different from the new terrorism of Al Qaeda, which will be examined in the following section.

New terrorism: Al Qaeda

Since the terrorist attacks against the United States on 11 September 2001, Al Qaeda has become nearly synonymous with terrorism and the terrorist threat. The group had emerged from the group of foreign fighters who had supported the mujahidin in their successful campaign against the Soviet occupation of Afghanistan in the 1980s. Initially, the term Al Qaeda, which was first used in 1988 and means 'the base', referred to some of the so-called Afghan Arabs who had gone through certain training camps and agreed to form part of an Islamic 'rapid reaction force' – ready to support local forces wherever Muslim lands were threatened by foreign invasion or occupation. At the time, little was known about the group, nor is it entirely clear whether all those who had been included in the original Al Qaeda were conscious that they had become members of a new group.[69]

In fact, to this day, government analysts disagree about the events that should be regarded as the first Al Qaeda attacks. The British government begins its Al Qaeda chronology with the first World Trade Center attacks in February 1993, followed by an incident in the Philippines in 1994[70] and the four-month bombing campaign carried out by Algerian Islamists in France in 1995.[71] The US State Department's *Global Patterns of Terrorism* report, on the other hand, starts with three bombings carried out in Yemen in December 1992 and the Black Hawk Down incident in Somalia in 1993 and lists no further attacks until the US Embassy bombings in East Africa in August 1998.[72]

Al Qaeda structures

The differing accounts of the group's origins reflect a deeper disagreement – apparently even between the two closest allies in the War on Terror – about what kind of structure Al Qaeda represents. In the period immediately following the 9/11 attacks, Al Qaeda was frequently portrayed as a hierarchical organization with a clear chain of command and control. Al Qaeda, it was argued, resembled a spider web, with Osama bin Laden at the centre and sleeper cells around the world, prepared to strike at western targets at any moment.[73] Quickly, this idea gave way to the notion of Al Qaeda as a 'franchise' operation. According to analysts such as Olivier Roy and Peter Bergen, rather than Al Qaeda itself being involved in the planning and carrying out of terrorist attacks, the Al Qaeda leadership merely sponsored acts of terrorism, subcontracting them to local groups who were given permission to take action on behalf of the wider movement.[74] Others believed that it was mistaken to understand Al Qaeda as a coherent organization at all. They argued that it represented an ideology which could be claimed by anyone who identified with certain beliefs. From this perspective, Al Qaeda was 'an amorphous [social] movement held together by a loosely networked transnational constituency'.[75]

The three images described here – spider web, franchise and social movement – are often portrayed as competing visions. In reality, though, they may *all* represent accurate understandings of Al Qaeda. In one of the best appreciations of the group, Jason Burke argues that Al Qaeda operates at three levels: the 'hard core' (also referred to as 'Al Qaeda Central'), consisting of bin Laden, his deputy and their lieutenants; the 'network', made up of mujahidin who took part in active jihad or spent longer periods in training camps in Afghanistan and Pakistan and have returned to their home countries; and the wider 'movement' of all those who identify with Al Qaeda ideology and are prepared to act on Al Qaeda Central's messages and instructions while having no direct association with its members and, at best, loose connections to the 'network'.[76]

Burke claims that the relationship between the three levels has never been static, and that the interplay between the various layers of the organization explains the changing dynamics of the movement. His observations are reflected in the writings of Abu Musab al Suri, one of Al Qaeda's leading military thinkers, who argued that the diffusion of the movement, which took place in the wake of the western invasion of Afghanistan in late 2001, has been a highly desirable development. According to al Suri, Al Qaeda was meant to be 'a system, not an organisation',[77] with the only link between the hard core and the wider movement being 'a common aim, a common doctrinal program and a . . . self-educational program'.[78]

Unsurprisingly, the diffuse nature of Al Qaeda has made it difficult for governments and analysts to understand its internal hierarchies and power structures. In particular, whereas many analysts believe that a relatively clear chain of command and control had existed prior to the western invasion of Afghanistan (where its leadership had been located), the extent to which the movement continues to be controlled from the top is subject to fierce debate. The former American official turned academic Marc Sageman, for instance, argues that – beginning in 2003 precisely – Al Qaeda has entered the phase of 'leaderless jihad' in which formal hierarchies no longer matter: 'Each local network carries out its attacks without coordination from above . . . [Al Qaeda] lacks a firm overarching strategy, [yet] it still has an agenda set by general guidelines found on the Internet, which is the virtual glue maintaining a weak appearance of unity.'[79] By contrast, Hoffman highlights recent intelligence assessments which demonstrate that Al Qaeda Central has regrouped in the tribal areas of Pakistan, reasserting some of the control which it had lost in recent years. Even where Islamist terror campaigns appear to be carried out by seemingly leaderless groups, such as in Europe, such activities had resulted from the 'deliberate, long-standing subversion by Al Qaeda'.[80] Many of the attempted terrorist plots in Europe, Hoffman points out, can be traced back to Pakistan, where members of the allegedly 'leaderless' jihad had received guidance, direction and training. Al Qaeda, he concludes, 'is a remarkably agile and flexible organization that exercises both top-down and bottom-up planning and operational capabilities'.[81]

As difficult as pinning down its command and control structures is the identification of Al Qaeda's centre of gravity. Though, historically, the group was dominated by Saudis and Egyptians (represented by the Saudi bin Laden and his Egyptian deputy, Ayman al Zawahiri, respectively), it now draws on recruits from across the world who often do not fight in their home countries. In Roy's view, Al Qaeda members should be seen as 'de-territorialized' in that, typically, 'the country where their family comes from, the country of residence and radicalization, and the country of action' are all different.[82] Furthermore, while Al Qaeda's activities coalesce in certain places, its focal point is constantly shifting. The group emerged through the confrontation with the Soviets in Afghanistan in the 1980s. In the 1990s, it focused on the conflicts in Bosnia, Chechnya and Kashmir. In the 2000s, the centre of gravity shifted from Afghanistan to Iraq and now seems to be reverting back to Afghanistan. In addition, Al Qaeda has continuously launched attacks against the so-called 'far enemy' – in particular, the United States – all over the globe, including in countries as diverse as Spain, Indonesia, Britain, Tanzania, and of course the United States itself. Both in terms of membership and organizational reach, therefore, Al Qaeda has become a truly transnational organization.

Al Qaeda aims

Al Qaeda's ideological agenda is as far-reaching as its organization. Simply put, the group aims to liberate and unite the global
community of Muslim believers (the *ummah*) whose rights and
interests it claims are being denied by a coalition of Christians
and Jews (the so-called Crusader and Zionist Alliance) as well
as apostate Muslim rulers. In Al Qaeda's view, faced with a
war against Islam, it is the individual duty of every Muslim to
defend the *ummah* through violence or 'armed struggle' (often
referred to as 'jihad').[83] The objective of jihad – as understood
by Al Qaeda – is to eliminate the obstacles that stand in the way
of creating a single Muslim nation (the caliphate) that would
be governed by shariah law and dominated by the strict social
practices derived from a literalist interpretation of the Koran
(often referred to as *Salafi* or *Wahhabi*).[84] In doing so, Al Qaeda
justifies violence against the secular regimes in the Middle
East, non-Muslim interests in the Muslim world, as well as
any outside influence that is judged to prevent the rise of the
ummah or contribute to the continued suppression, exploitation and occupation of the Muslim world.[85]

In recent years, it has become controversial to say in public
that Al Qaeda and its ideology have anything to do with religion
and Islam in particular. The British Home Secretary, Jacqui
Smith, even went as far as saying that, instead of referring to
'Islamic terrorism', Al Qaeda's attacks should be described
as 'un-Islamic terrorism'.[86] This may be correct in that the
views espoused by Al Qaeda and its followers have little to do
with mainstream Islamic scholarship, nor do they reflect the
religious views held by the vast majority of Muslims across the
globe. It is also true that bin Laden's appeal in some parts of
the Muslim world is not based on deep religious conviction but
stems, to a large extent, from the political grievances he articu-
lates. Still, Al Qaeda and its ideology would make little sense if
one were to eliminate the religious element altogether. From Al

Qaeda's perspective, religion is not merely a powerful tool that helps to mobilize a constituency but it sanctions the use of violence and defines the movement's political agenda. Although Al Qaeda's aims and objectives may be political in the sense of being this-worldly, the source of its activism, its purpose and justification are undoubtedly religious. Accordingly, the Italian academic Sara Silvestri described radical Islam as a 'political theology': it derives 'its driving reasons, symbols, and language from Islam in order to theorize a variety of degrees and methods of political mobilisation and to bring about Islamisation and political change'.[87]

An entirely different argument postulates that there are 'striking parallels' between ideologies of Al Qaeda and the anti-globalization Left. The British philosopher John Gray believes that many supporters of Al Qaeda should be more accurately described as 'Islamo-Leninists' than 'Islamo-fascists'.[88] Likewise, Roy argues that Al Qaeda's ideological 'origins and those of the modern western current of anti-imperialism are similar. It is common to find among Islamic radicals a mix of Koranic injunctions and pseudo-Marxist explanations.'[89] And indeed, the anti-globalization Left and Al Qaeda seem to have plenty of enemies in common, not least neo-liberal capitalism, American hegemony and Israel. Bin Laden's views on the United States – condemning western consumerism, the exploitation of the global South, the Vietnam war and so on[90] – often read more like a Trotskyite pamphlet than the statement of a self-styled religious leader. Even so, there remain very substantial differences which must not be ignored. Whatever one thinks of the anti-globalization movement, its vision for the future is rooted in universalist values such as human rights, gender equality and participatory democracy. Al Qaeda's proposed solution, on the other hand, lies in the construction of a particularist theocracy which upholds the supremacy of Islam, promotes medieval social norms and is opposed to democracy or any other form of 'man-made law'.[91] While participation in both movements may be driven by the same 'rebellious', anti-system impulse,[92] the ideas underlying the political programmes of Al Qaeda and the anti-globalization Left are diametrically opposed.

Al Qaeda methods

When trying to determine the nature and extent of Al Qaeda's violence – the third variable – it becomes clear how difficult and confusing it can be to deal with a highly diffuse global movement such as Al Qaeda. When counting the number of casualties, does one consider only the attacks organized by Al Qaeda Central, or also those carried out by local groups? Is it sufficient to look at the groups that openly identify with Al Qaeda (Al Qaeda in Iraq, Al Qaeda in the Islamic Maghreb, etc.) or should those that merely embrace its ideology be included as well? While it may be difficult to present any data that would be entirely incontestable, the tendency for Al Qaeda or Al Qaeda-inspired groups to engage in acts of mass-casualty terrorism is beyond doubt. Drawing on the RAND/ MIPT Terrorism Incident database and using the widest possible definition of 'jihadist terrorism',[93] the two American journalists Peter Bergen and Paul Cruickshank have counted 731 incidents causing 6,586 fatalities in the five years following the September 11 attacks in 2001. This amounts to an average of nine fatalities for every attack. Excluding the insurgencies in Iraq and Afghanistan, the tendency becomes even more pronounced: Bergen and Cruickshank count 170 attacks resulting in 2,662 casualties, which equates to an average of nearly 16 fatalities for every attack.[94]

Going through the lists of Al Qaeda-related incidents put together by the American and British governments (which, admittedly, exclude attacks in Afghanistan and Iraq),[95] it becomes obvious that the vast majority of targets were chosen precisely in order to maximize civilian casualties. Examples include the attacks against tourists visiting a synagogue in Tunisia in April 2002 which killed 21; the killing of more than 200 tourists and workers in Bali in October 2002; the attacks against a Spanish club and a hotel in Casablanca in May 2003 that resulted in 45 fatalities; the bombings of synagogues and British institutions in Istanbul in November 2003, killing over 60 people; the Madrid train attacks in March 2004, leaving 191 commuters dead; the bombing of tourist sites in Egypt in October 2004, which killed more than 30; and the London transport attacks in July 2005, which killed 52.

A smaller percentage of Al Qaeda attacks have been directed against targets that could be rationalized as related to enemy governments, but where no care was taken to avoid the death of innocent bystanders. This refers to incidents such as the truck bomb attacks against the US consulate in Karachi, which killed 12; or the car bomb placed outside the Australian embassy in September 2004, which resulted in nine deaths. Only a small fraction of Al Qaeda attacks in the post-9/11 period can be said to have followed a rationale in which the targeting of civilians – either as a primary consideration or as a secondary effect – played no role at all. (The bombing of the French oil tanker *Limburg* off the Yemen cost in October 2002 is one example.) Moreover, in none of the cases listed is there any indication that warnings had been issued prior to the attacks.

The evidence presented here ties in well with Al Qaeda leaders' writings and statements which underscore the group's determination to engage in unprecedented levels of violence. In his most important book, *Knights under the Prophet's Banner*, Al Zawahiri highlights the need for Al Qaeda to 'escalate its methods of strikes . . . for this is the language understood by the West'.[96] It may come as no surprise, then, that there have been numerous attempts by Al Qaeda and its associated groups to acquire CBRN materials. It is well established, for example, that Al Qaeda experimented with biological and chemical substances in its training camps in Afghanistan prior to the western invasion in late 2001, and that the group's leaders have expressed their desire to obtain nuclear weapons and frequently threatened their enemies with CBRN attacks.[97] While the likelihood of such attacks can easily be exaggerated, Al Qaeda's track record, its ideology and stated intentions suggest that what stops the group are not so much ethical constraints but, rather, the difficulty of acquiring and disseminating the necessary materials. In contrast to the IRA, then, it may be reasonable to suppose that Al Qaeda would not hesitate to use CBRN materials if they could be obtained and made to work.

The purpose of this chapter was to capture and illustrate how terrorism has evolved from 'old' to 'new'. Significant change could be observed in three areas:

- *The diffusion of terrorist group structures.* Whereas terrorist groups tended to be highly formalized structures, hierarchical relationships have made way for loose networks that are flatter and based largely on personal relationships. Also, rather than revolving around one centre of gravity, terrorist groups can be transnational actors that have no permanent geographical point of reference and draw their recruits from all over the world.
- *The rise of religiously inspired ideologies.* Religious ideologies may not have entirely replaced nationalism, but they now play a far greater role in inspiring terrorist campaigns than anyone would have predicted just thirty years ago. This reflects a broader trend which has seen the revival of religious and religiously inspired political movements across the world.

- *The greater lethality and brutality of terrorist operations.* While terrorist attacks used to be aimed at targets that could be associated with enemy governments and their representatives, terrorists now routinely target civilian populations, hoping to produce mass-casualty incidents. This tendency is reflected also in the greater brutality with which terrorist operations are carried out.

The two case studies presented in this chapter – Al Qaeda and the IRA – are meant to illustrate rather than substantiate the two concepts because they contain most of the characteristics of old and new terrorism respectively. Admittedly, the majority of terrorist groups are more difficult to categorize. Hamas, for example, is a religiously inspired group which has carried out mass-casualty attacks and whose structures are somewhat networked,[98] but there is little to suggest that it would ever be inclined to 'go transnational'.[99] Similarly, the Tamil Tigers have been involved in mass-casualty attacks, yet their political programme is strictly secular and limited to 'liberating' what they regard as their homeland. Should those groups be regarded as old or new?

As pointed out in the first chapter, the transformation from old to new terrorism has neither been uniform nor universal. While most terrorist groups have been affected – in some way or another – by the powerful forces that have triggered the rise of the new terrorism, this does not mean that they have all become religiously driven, mass-casualty producing networks. Indeed, in the majority of cases, it seems as if existing groups have adopted aspects of the new terrorism while resisting others.

This does not invalidate the concepts that have been described. On the contrary, the mapping out of 'ideal types' (see Figure 2.1) makes it possible to understand where individual groups are located on the evolutionary spectrum, and whether and to what extent they have been affected by the influences that will be described in the remaining parts of this book. Very rarely are the answers clear-cut, but it is precisely as a methodology for disaggregating the different characteristics of the phenomenon that the ideas of old and new terrorism can help in grasping how terrorism and/or terrorist groups have changed. As mentioned in the first chapter, rather than thinking in absolutes, it may be more accurate therefore to speak of new*er* and old*er* terrorism.

The key question this chapter has not answered is what caused the change from old to new. What, in other words, is the nature of the 'powerful forces' that were hinted at earlier? The evolution of terrorism over the past decades cannot be explained without reference to the processes that are said to be part of globalization and late modernity. Inevitably, the reality is more complex than saying 'globalization caused terrorism,' but there can be no question that the conditions associated with late modernity and globalization represent crucial variables without which many of the developments that were outlined in this chapter make no sense. The following chapters attempt to show how late modernity and globalization have contributed to the rise of network structures and transnational orientations; how they have facilitated the revival of religiously inspired ideologies; and how they can explain the trend towards greater brutality and lethality in modern terrorism.

CHAPTER THREE

Holy War, Inc.? The Emergence of Transnational Terror Networks

When Al Qaeda struck the United States, Peter Bergen, the investigative journalist who interviewed Osama bin Laden in his cave in Afghanistan in the late 1990s, was putting the finishing touches to his book about the world's most wanted terrorist. *Holy War, Inc.* was published soon after the September 11 attacks,[1] and it argued that bin Laden had created an entirely new type of terrorist organization. Earlier than most, Bergen recognized that bin Laden – while embracing a seemingly medieval interpretation of the world – had consciously exploited 'entirely modern sensibilities and technologies' in order to wage war against the very forces which had brought these sensibilities and technologies into being.[2] Not only was bin Laden using satellite phones and (increasingly) the Internet, Al Qaeda as a whole looked like a transnational conglomerate of which bin Laden served as the chief executive.[3]

This chapter examines the reasons behind the diffusion of terrorist structures which Bergen so aptly described. It argues that globalization has been central to the whole process through which hierarchical organizations have turned into seemingly chaotic, transnational networks. The first section takes a closer look at the different layers of responsibility within terrorist groups and explains how two of the dynamics that are often thought to be critical to the process of globalization – the 'information revolution' and the freer movement of people across national borders – have helped to alter their respective roles and relationships. The second section investigates the rise of transnationalism. Here again, two developments that are widely seen as important aspects of globalization – the spread of new technologies and the consequences of global migration – are singled out for having played a crucial role in facilitating the transformation from old to new.

The networking of terrorism

As early as 1997, the American academic Jessica Matthews argued that information technology had prompted the rise of 'decentralized networks' which would challenge states' monopoly of power: 'Businesses, citizens' organizations, ethnic groups, and crime cartels have all readily adopted the network model. Governments, on the other hand, are quintessential hierarchies, wedded to an organization form incompatible with all that the new technologies makes possible.'[4] Fifteen years later, the journalist Fareed Zakaria explained what this meant for the future of violence. In his book *The Future of Freedom*, he claimed that globalization and information technology had 'democratized' the use of violence. Through the Internet, 'almost anyone can get his hands on anything . . . Today, if you want to find sources for anthrax, recipes for poison, or methods to weaponize chemicals, all you need is a good search engine.'[5]

Matthews and Zakaria captured many of the drivers that have made the diffusion of terrorist structures possible. It is important, however, not to overstate their impact or oversimplify the way in which the process has unfolded. Take, for example, the argument that globalization and information technology have undermined the power of the state. There can be no doubt, of course, that state sponsorship, which in one form or another used to be essential in making terrorist groups effective, is less significant than it used to be. Nevertheless, it would be mistaken to believe that the rise of 'decentralized networks' has made such support irrelevant. As the American academic Daniel Byman points out, those who dismiss 'a focus on states as unimportant or "old think"' are ignoring some of the world's most successful terrorist groups (such as Hezbollah and Hamas) who continue to rely on state sponsors. In general, it seems obvious that, even in the so-called network age, government support can enhance terrorist groups' capabilities by transforming rag-tag armies into well-trained, well-equipped fighting forces with access to funds and territory.[6]

Likewise, it is a common error to believe that 'mostly what you need is knowledge',[7] and that, consequently, the wider availability of information through the Internet has caused the proliferation of terrorist violence. In reality, information on how to construct explosives or even nuclear bombs was available long before the Internet was invented. Johann Most, a German Anarchist who emigrated to the United States, wrote and published a booklet on how to build bombs in the late nineteenth century which also served as the principal inspiration for *The Anarchist Cookbook* that circulated among radical Leftists in the 1960s and 1970s.[8] Similarly, instructions on how to construct nuclear, chemical or biological weapons are not just available from the Internet but can be found in most university libraries.

What Zakaria fails to recognize is that effective terrorism requires not only information but also experience, skill, resources and some degree of strategic direction. Information technology, therefore, matters not just because it provides access to bomb-making instructions and poison recipes but, more importantly, because it enables terrorists to communicate and coordinate in ways that had hitherto been unimaginable. The novelty lies not simply in the wider availability of information but the greater degree, scope and speed of interactivity that have become possible. Combined with the freer movement of people and capital, this has produced a situation in which traditional hierarchies are no longer necessary or efficient and – as will be shown – the roles and modus operandi of terrorist leaderships, 'middle management' and grassroots have been fundamentally redefined.

Leaderships

Globalization has empowered terrorist leaderships to perform functions that are radically different from the ones their predecessors carried out. Whereas during the era of old terrorism, leaderships were involved in all aspects of the terrorist campaign, including the day-to-day running of operations, globalization compels leaderships to concentrate on strategic issues, such as the setting of the broad parameters within which the campaign ought to be conducted and the communication with supporters and sympathizers. Like the board of a multinational corporation, terrorist leaderships are removed from much of the operational business and, instead, focus on strategic guidance and expanding the movement. It may still be difficult to imagine a situation in which – as the right-wing strategist Louis Beam put it – 'no one need issue an order to anyone',[9] but there can be little doubt that the conditions in which (near-) 'leaderless resistance' could materialize have improved dramatically.

In no other area is the changing role of terrorist leaderships more obvious than communication. One of the principal reasons why the vision of purely inspirational leadership could not be made to work when Beam coined the idea of 'leaderless resistance' is that there were few, if any, channels through which leaders could communicate with (and, thus, inspire) their followers. Where a society did not permit the free transmission of information, it was impossible for radical movements to advertise their vision of a new society to a broader audience of sympathizers and potential supporters, as all the channels of mass communication were controlled by the authorities. Even in democracies, the vast bulk of the media tended to be concentrated in the hands of a few media entrepreneurs who had – by and large – benefited from the status quo and were unlikely to be interested in alienating their governments by providing extremists with a platform.[10] This is not to say that leaderships could not communicate with their sympathizers. But they mostly relied on traditional methods such as personal appearances and the distribution of leaflets and audio cassettes which were slow and cumbersome and exposed those involved to considerable risks. Even Timothy McVeigh, the Oklahoma bomber, who – in many respects – fitted the description of the 'leaderless resister', still relied on underground newsletters and the infamous novel, *The Turner Diaries*, for inspiration.[11]

One development which helped terrorist leaderships become more effective in reaching their audience was the rise of satellite television, especially in the Arab world. Until the mid-1990s, people in most Middle Eastern countries typically had access to the programmes of up to a handful of television stations which were all state-owned or state-licensed. In either case, the governments could control what people were allowed to see because they were in charge of the (terrestrial) means through which these programmes were distributed. The emergence of satellite television led to an explosion of channels which could no longer be regulated by national governments because the stations' headquarters were located outside the governments' jurisdictions and the means of distribution could no longer be 'switched off'. Compared to 1990, when there existed only one Arabic satellite channel with a few thousand viewers in the Gulf states, by 2007, nearly 300 million Arabs had access to satellite television, with more than 200 channels broadcasting in the Arabic language ('second only to the number of satellite channels in English').[12]

Some of the satellite channels currently broadcasting to Arab audiences are openly sympathetic to radical causes. The Lebanese group Hezbollah, for example, runs the television station *Al Manar,* which can be seen via satellite across the Middle East. Though some believe that its influence has been overrated,[13] *Al Manar* is widely known and has a stable audience (according to some accounts, it is the fourth most popular satellite news station in the Middle East) and it represents one of the Arabs' key sources for information on the Israel–Palestine conflict.[14] More importantly, even where satellite channels are not explicitly committed to promoting a terrorist group or its ideology, terrorist leaderships now deal with journalistic interlocutors whose decisions are less restrained by government policy. Popular television channels like *Al Jazeera* are undoubtedly freer than traditional, state-owned television to broadcast the statements of bin Laden or his deputy, Ayman al Zawahiri, whenever they consider them to be significant or of interest to their audience. Hence, whereas two decades ago it would have been inconceivable for Zawahiri to appear on Egyptian television screens inciting his fellow countrymen to overthrow their government, there is no longer anything the Egyptian regime can do to prevent this from happening.

The most dramatic development, however, has been the rise of the Internet which has enabled terrorist leaderships to cut out the journalistic 'middlemen' altogether.[15] Some of the recently published studies about the use of the Internet by Al Qaeda and its affiliated groups emphasize how extensively the Internet has come to be used by terrorist leaderships and how central they believe its role to be. Indeed, as early as 2001, Zawahiri wrote that the Internet was key to 'get[ting] our message across to the masses and break[ing] the media siege imposed on the jihad movement'.[16] In the following years, the movement built a virtual infrastructure that has permitted the instant publication of statements, explanations, clarifications as well as the production and distribution of video clips and announcements.[17] Recent statements by Al Qaeda leaders, for example, were no longer released via *Al Jazeera* but posted on the most prominent jihadist web forums.

Not only has the Internet enabled leaderships to incite their followers and issue strategic guidance on what countries and targets should be operational priorities, it has allowed sympathizers to become active participants in the discussion about the direction of the movement. This has made leaderships more responsive and – to some extent – accountable to their followers, even when they are thousands of miles apart. Indeed, the Internet – by virtue of being interactive – has introduced an element of 'democracy' which has permitted more people to become part of the debate and challenge their leaderships.[18] Leaders, in other words, can no longer take it for granted that their guidance is interpreted as it was intended and that their instructions are followed as they were issued. The Internet, then, while presenting terrorist leaderships with new and virtually unlimited opportunities for disseminating their message and inspiring sympathizers to become part of the movement, may simultaneously undermine their absolute authority.

Another consequence of globalization for how terrorist groups are being led has been the loosening of spatial constraints. Put simply, terrorist leaderships no longer have to be in the same geographical place as their followers. Through information technology – cell and satellite phones as well as email and the Internet – it has become possible not just to communicate with followers but to transfer documents and resources with little chance of detection. In terms of communicating with members or followers, it no longer matters a great deal if the leadership's headquarters are in a neighbouring country, thousands of miles away, or whether there are no physical headquarters at all. More specifically, information technology, combined with cheaper international travel, has enabled terrorist leaderships to establish their bases in less developed countries with weak or near-absent law enforcement or judicial structures. In the era of old terrorism, the remoteness and lack of infrastructure in such countries would have made it difficult to run effective terrorist campaigns. But, as Al Qaeda has demonstrated, even the most dramatic acts of terrorism can now be directed from places as remote and seemingly underdeveloped as Afghanistan.

Byman is correct in noting that most terrorist groups – even those widely claimed not to receive any state support – still have relationships with states.[19] At the same time, it should be pointed out that the nature of that relationship has changed as spatial constraints have loosened. In the 1970s and 1980s, one of the key principles of counter-terrorism doctrine used to be that no terrorist group could survive without a state sponsor, and that, consequently, punishing those states which supported terrorist groups was the most effective means of containing terrorism.[20] Even then, this was, at best, simplistic and mostly did not work.[21] More recently, the increased ability of terrorist groups to spread across, and move between, states has not only strengthened their bargaining position vis-à-vis states, it has also made the idea of punishing host or sponsoring states even less plausible. As shown above, terrorist groups can take advantage of weak states which – as in the case of Afghanistan – might become as dependent on the terrorists' support as vice versa.[22] In fact, Al Qaeda has moved its headquarters on at least three occasions and, though much weakened, none of these 'moves' have destroyed the organization altogether.[23]

However, increased mobility and 'stretching' come at a price. Terrorist leaderships can incite their sympathizers in faraway countries through video messages and web forums, while information technology makes it possible to keep in touch with key operators via phone and email. But their ability to run campaigns – that is, to direct attacks and engage in operational planning – is severely limited by distance and the resulting loss of personal interaction. The leadership may issue all kinds of strategic guidance but, as pointed out earlier, whether and how this is followed is largely beyond their control. Again, Al Qaeda provides the best example: when the leader of Al Qaeda in Iraq, Abu Musab al Zarqawi, was beginning to carry out his (hugely unpopular) strategy of igniting a civil war between Sunnis and Shiites in Iraq, Zawahiri could neither call off the campaign nor could he discipline Zarqawi. All he was able to do was to write a letter in which he reminded Zarqawi that successful jihad required a minimum of popular support and that slaughtering Shiites would be unhelpful.[24] Needless to say, Zarqawi ignored the advice.

'Middle management'

The main burden of running terrorist campaigns in the era of new terrorism falls to the 'middle management', that is, local leaders and more experienced activists who traditionally would have assisted the leadership in carrying out specialized tasks. In the old terrorism model, such individuals would have contributed to the decision-making process by offering their ideas and initiative, and it would have been common for them to be consulted on all kinds of matters, ranging from the technical feasibility of certain operations to gauging the likely reactions of the group's constituency. Ultimately, though, decisions would have been taken by their superiors. Only the leaders or their ruling body could authorize particular operations or, say, a change in policy to allow the bombing of people or places that had hitherto been off limits. In cases in which middle managers persisted in pursuing policies or actions that contradicted the leadership's wishes, there would have been mechanisms of internal discipline to ensure that members could be reprimanded, expelled or otherwise punished. Hence, while having some input into the decision-making process, the role of the middle management was to follow orders and 'make things happen' rather than question the policies adopted by their superiors.

Under the new terrorism model, middle managers enjoy greater freedom in pursuing their own agendas without much interference from the top, but they are also expected to take on far greater responsibilities. For the reasons outlined above, leaderships may no longer be willing or capable of managing their organizations to the extent to which this was possible under the old terrorism model. Instead of relying on precise instructions, middle managers now need to interpret the leadership's pronouncements, judge their applicability and context, and translate them into operations on the ground. Given the cacophony of voices in places such as the Internet, it is for the middle managers to generate consensus or at least identify those voices who carry more weight than others. Having established what needs to be done, it is their responsibility to build and maintain a following. They also have to accumulate operational resources, such as finance and training, often with little support from the leadership. In essence, then, middle managers are expected to become local 'entrepreneurs' who will take matters into their own hands and build micro-organizations while maintaining links to the leadership and into the wider network.[25]

The processes associated with globalization have made it easier for middle managers to accomplish these tasks. In particular, while access to the leadership may be difficult, opportunities for maintaining links across the network have been dramatically improved as a result of information technology, freer travel and the way in which societies have changed as a result of global migration. In the case of Al Qaeda, for instance, it may well be true that the network was brought into existence as a result of the anti-Soviet jihad in Afghanistan in the 1980s and the personal relationships between foreign fighters that formed during that period (see chapter 2), but it could not have survived and remained operational without cheap and easy travel which permitted its members to meet, congregate and coalesce after they had returned to their respective home countries. The preparation for all Al Qaeda operations against the West, such as the September 11 attacks, involved significant amounts of international phone calls, 'dozens of international trips' and meetings with individuals from numerous countries.[26] Furthermore, as the final report of the so-called 9/11 Commission (which was given the task of investigating the intelligence failure leading to the attacks) demonstrated, members of the network rarely aroused any suspicion because they blended into migrant and diaspora communities which did not exist forty or fifty years ago.[27]

In principle, it is possible to imagine that such networks could have existed in earlier periods, but the speed, intensity and low cost of interaction that have become possible as a result of globalization have dramatically lowered the threshold for their emergence.[28] In fact, one may argue that, in operating these networks, the terrorist middle managers are taking advantage of the same principles and doctrines that have underpinned the logic of free trade, which has permitted greater economies of scale and let corporate entities operate more efficiently by widening the pool of available resources. Hence, terrorist groups' middle managers are no longer constrained by national boundaries or geographical distance in drawing together the resources that are necessary in order to carry out an operation. Instead of relying on local talent, they may bring in experienced individuals from abroad who can help in carrying out specialized tasks, such as the production of explosives, or organize training sessions in countries in which the security environment is lax. Furthermore, as with multinational corporations, the place in which the 'product' is 'sold' (that is, the place in which the terrorist attack is being carried out) may no longer bear any relation to the multitude of places that were involved in its 'production' (that is, the places in which the operation was planned, financed and organized).

An excellent illustration of how middle managers have taken over the running of terrorist campaigns and how, in doing so, they are drawing on the opportunities made possible by globalization are the Madrid train bombings on 11 March 2004 that killed 191 people. The Madrid network evolved out of a group of Syrian jihadists that had settled in Spain after fleeing or being expelled from their home country. They were led by Imad Eddin Yarkas, better known as Abu Dahdah, who had established contacts among senior Al Qaeda members across Europe and the Middle East.[29] One of his closest associates in the late 1990s was Abu Qatada, a Jordanian-born cleric who was based in London and has frequently been referred to by law enforcement and security agencies as bin Laden's 'ambassador' to Europe.[30] According to the Spanish police, over a period of five years, Abu Dahdah and Abu Qatada saw each other on seventeen occasions.[31] The purpose of their meetings was to discuss fundraising, to help with the distribution of videos and promotional materials in Spain and to assist with the transfer of local recruits from Spain to various jihadist battlefronts (especially Chechnya and Bosnia) and the Al Qaeda training camps in Afghanistan.[32] Abu Dahdah was particularly successful in recruiting North African immigrants, including a young Moroccan named Amer Azizi who was to assume a central position in forming the group that carried out the Madrid attacks.

Abu Dahdah, who was arrested by the Spanish police in the wake of the September 11 attacks, exemplified the persona of the middle manager. Relentless in his efforts to expand the jihadist movement in Spain, he also went to great lengths to try to maintain his links with the wider network, thus ensuring that the growing numbers of recruits were integrated – however loosely – into Al Qaeda. As a result, though none of the individuals who were directly involved in the Madrid attacks had ever attended an Al Qaeda training camp or met with any member of the Al Qaeda leadership, they clearly believed themselves to be acting on behalf of Al Qaeda. They all had consumed copious amounts of Al Qaeda propaganda materials, referred to bin Laden as their *emir*[33] and appeared to act on the strategic guidance provided by the Al Qaeda leadership. When bin Laden, in a video message in October 2003, threatened Spain with retaliation for its participation in the occupation of Iraq, one of the leaders of the Madrid network entered 'March 11' as his birthday on his mobile phone. Two months later, a well-known jihadist web site released a 'strategy document' which made the case for a terrorist attack against Spanish troops in Iraq. Another paper, which explicitly encouraged attacks within Spain, was published days later.[34] It is still not known whether any of the members of the Madrid cell ever received a direct 'order' to launch the attack, but it seems clear that they were under the impression that this was what Al Qaeda Central wanted.

The Madrid network was extensive, and many of the linkages and connections between individual members and the wider network continue to be unexplored. Azizi, for example, had relations with the Moroccan Islamic Combatant Group and the Libyan Islamic Fighting Group. One of his recruits, Mustapha Al Maymouni, set up jihadist cells in both Spain and Morocco, travelling frequently between the two countries. When Al Maymouni was arrested in connection with the Casablanca attacks in 2003, his place was taken by a Tunisian, Serhane Fakhet. Fakhet recruited a former member of the

Armed Islamic Group from Algeria, as well as a Moroccan drug trafficker whose business provided much of the funds that were needed to launch the operation. Meanwhile, two Spanish citizens of Syrian origin, Moutaz and Mohannad Almallah, managed to re-establish a connection with Abu Qatada's associates in London.[35] In fact, according to newspaper reports, Fakhet had his own connection with a radical preacher in London whom he phoned on the day he and six other members of the group committed suicide.[36] Much remains uncertain about the ways in which the network drew on the resources of its international partners, but the extent to which its leaders were linked across Europe and North Africa highlights quite how insignificant national borders had become for them. Most importantly, it demonstrates the role of middle managers in making fairly complex operations such as the Madrid bombings work.

Grassroots

The changing roles played by terrorist leaderships and middle management have had significant consequences for those at the bottom of the hierarchy. If the journalist Thomas Friedman is correct in arguing that globalization has broken down traditional hierarchies by providing individuals with better tools to organize, mobilize and make their voices heard,[37] terrorist groups may find it easier to assert themselves in relation to states or whoever else they claim to fight. Based on this argument, one could contend that, *within* such groups, the breaking down of hierarchies described by Friedman has led to a shift in power away from the leadership and the middle managers to the grassroots. This, indeed, is the hypothesis presented by many scholars and analysts who have coined a barrage of terms to describe what they believe to be a fundamental transformation in the way in which terrorist groups function. Following some of the Al Qaeda-inspired attacks in recent years, they speak of self-starters, self-radicalization, self-mobilization, self-recruitment and self-activation.[38]

In the argument about 'super-empowered grassroots',[39] the Internet plays a pivotal role because – in theory at least – the entire process of radicalization and recruitment no longer needs to take place in a real-world group context. Propaganda materials are available online and web forums have enabled radicalized individuals to find each other with no risk of being exposed to the authorities: terrorist cells can form online with no need for any active recruitment by leaders or middle managers. Once a decision has been taken to go operational, the self-starters can download training manuals and instructions on how to build bombs, making the involvement of any organized structure in the planning process obsolete. Should they wish to be associated with any organization, they may decide to follow the group's strategic guidance that is available on the Internet. Equally, though, they may choose to ignore the leadership altogether. Since cells are entirely independent and there exists no direct link between the leadership and the grassroots, they enjoy complete freedom in choosing the timing and targets of their attacks. Considering the possibilities for autonomous organization and mobilization that have thus become available, it may be no surprise that even as respected a scholar as Marc Sageman has fully bought into the idea of 'leaderless jihad', with the Internet – rather than the leaders or middle managers – being the 'virtual glue' that holds terrorist networks together (see chapter 2).[40]

The argument seems compelling, but one has to be careful not to overstate the notion of self-starters and, especially, the idea that the Internet has made leaders and middle managers redundant. In general, although terrorist cells often appear to be genuine self-starters or 'amateurs' at first, once the plots have been fully investigated it frequently turns out that they had links with a network. The perpetrators of the Madrid attacks, for example, were initially described as self-starters, but it quickly became obvious that their leaders had been extensively connected with Al Qaeda structures in Europe and North Africa (see above, pp. 60–2). The same is true for the London transport bombers and the so-called Hofstad group in the Netherlands (one of whose members assassinated the filmmaker Theo van Gogh). The latter was originally described as a nihilistic street gang with no structure and formalized recruitment, but is now believed to have been a highly networked, ideologically conscious group with extensive international links.[41]

Furthermore, there can be no doubt that the Internet has transformed the way in which terrorist groups function but, as much as promoting autonomy, this new medium can also be said to have facilitated self-starters' integration into wider network structures. Most wannabe terrorists do not resent being part of an organization. Rather, they often turn to the Internet precisely in order to seek links with existing networks so they can become part of a greater cause and receive professional training. Take, for example, the case of Younis Tsouli, better known as 'irhabi007' ('terrorist007'), who emerged as the 'superstar' of jihadism online in early 2004. Tsouli had joined a number of popular jihadist web forums and quickly gained recognition because of his expertise in hacking computer systems.[42] Within a matter of months, he had become one of the most important hubs for the jihadist online community. Crucially, he not only managed the flow of information among grassroots jihadists, but maintained contacts with the middle managers of militant groups from across Europe, North America and the Middle East and is said to have brokered 'links to the jihad' for a number of self-starters. Hence, far from advancing the idea of 'leaderless jihad', he actually served as a matchmaker who allowed self-starters to join more formalized structures.[43]

In fact, the only terrorist movement with fully empowered grassroots is not Al Qaeda but the Earth Liberation Front (ELF), which was established in the English city of Brighton in 1992 and was initially believed to represent the 'militant wing' of the environmental organization *Earth First!* By the mid-1990s, ELF had gone its own way and operational links with *Earth First!* were no longer thought to be of great significance. The group has mostly engaged in acts of vandalism and arson that were targeted against institutions associated with environmental destruction and exploitation, such as multinational corporations and research laboratories as well as the construction and tourism industries. Though no one has yet been killed, ELF has caused considerable economic damage. The group is believed to have been responsible for 600 criminal acts between 1996 and 2002,[44] including the burning down of a ski resort in Colorado which resulted in $12 million of damage. In 2003, it set fire to an apartment building in San Diego, which caused a loss of $50 million. A senior FBI official described 'eco-terrorism' in the form of ELF as 'the No. 1 domestic terrorism threat' in 2005.[45]

ELF has no central organization, and there are no links between the different cells responsible for attacks. Indeed, there are no efforts to facilitate or encourage such links on behalf of the group's 'leadership'. On the contrary, in a promotional video, one of ELF's publicists makes it clear that 'there's no realistic chance of becoming active in an already existing cell . . . Take initiative; form your own cell'.[46] The 'leadership' never gets involved in any operational planning or decisions about targeting. It sees its role primarily in issuing basic guidelines and principles according to which it then claims and publicizes successful actions as part of the ELF campaign. It also publishes advice on how to carry out operations and maximize their impact. Initially, the primary means through which such guidance was communicated was the telephone and (then) email.[47] Only the rise of the World Wide Web, however, has made the group's organizational model fully viable. It could be argued that the Internet now represents the group's 'centre of gravity' around which the entire campaign revolves. It is through their publication on ELF web sites that seemingly isolated acts of vandalism and sabotage are connected, recognized and become part of a larger campaign. In fact, it seems reasonable to speculate that, without publication on the Internet, many of the group's low-level acts of violence would probably go unnoticed; and with no recognition by a broader – albeit virtual – constituency, many of those engaged in the group as 'leaderless resisters' might lose interest and have no real incentive to carry on.

The ELF campaign illustrates the potential for grassroots-driven mobilization in the Internet era, but it also reveals some of its limitations. First, the lack of any form of command and control structures makes it practically impossible for the group to implement a coherent strategy or develop the momentum that would be needed in order to achieve strategic impact. Whether, where and when attacks are carried out is decided by chance rather than by careful planning and coordination from the top. Certain industries and causes are highlighted on the group's web site, presumably in order to steer supporters in particular directions. At the same time, the publicists are careful never to incite violence against specific targets for fear of this being used as a pretext for shutting down their web site.[48] If ELF could count on thousands of cells across the world, there might be a chance that the cumulative effect of their actions, however uncoordinated, could lead to a degree of terror and panic among corporate elites. However, with just a few active cells spread across the world, it seems rather unlikely that the possibility of being attacked by ELF will ever influence any major investment decision. Against this background, the FBI's assessment of ELF as the 'No. 1

domestic terrorism threat' should be interpreted as evidence of quite how little there was to fear from domestic terrorism in the United States until recently.

The second limitation of the grassroots-driven model is the lack of capabilities possessed by most 'amateur' terrorists. Most of the criminal acts that are carried out by ELF supporters are low-level acts of vandalism, such as graffiti. The most damaging tactic that has been used by ELF is arson which, as described above, has caused considerable damage on a number of occasions. The group has never blown anything up, nor do the group's manuals explain or encourage the use of explosives. Partly, this may be an effort to distance itself from 'ordinary' terrorists. It is more likely, though, that the leadership has recognized that the construction of bombs requires a degree of expertise, and that ELF's supporters – mostly young men, often in their teens or early twenties[49] – would probably cause more harm to themselves than to any of their targets in attempting to produce such devices. Needless to say, there are some notable exceptions of leaderless resisters who possessed considerable operational skills, for example Timothy McVeigh, the Oklahoma bomber, who together with an associate managed to assemble a large fertilizer-based bomb and place it in exactly the spot where it was likely to cause maximum damage. In general, though, grassroots-driven groups lack the professional skills and expertise to pull off spectaculars such as the September 11 attacks or even the Madrid or London transport bombings.

Overall, therefore, one may conclude that the characterization of the new terrorism as an exclusively grassroots-driven phenomenon is only partially true. Rather, the rise of the new terrorism has prompted changes in the roles and responsibilities of *all* the tiers that exist within terrorist organizations. Information technology and freer travel have provided leaderships with new opportunities for communication and the ability to overcome spatial constraints (thereby improving their chances of survival even in the most adverse circumstances), whilst their ability to run day-to-day operations has been limited. In turn, globalization and the processes associated with it have empowered the middle managers of terrorism whose ability to network and draw on resources across borders has effectively turned them into semi-independent entrepreneurs with great freedoms but also increased burdens. By contrast, purely grassroots-driven campaigns continue to suffer from a lack of strategic coherence and capabilities. How these developments relate to the rise of 'transnationalism' will be explored in the following section.

The emergence of transnationalism

When looking at the reasons behind the rise of transnationalism and transnational terrorist structures in particular, some of the explanations sound fairly obvious. As early as 1987, for example, the American academics John Meyer, John Boli and George Thomas highlighted the impact of new communication technologies, which have enabled the rapid exchange of information across countries, as well as the availability of cheap international travel, which has made it possible for activists to overcome spatial constraints and build personal relationships in spite of great distances. Significantly, they also point to the diffusion of English as the 'lingua franca of a new age'.[50] In the twenty years since they published their article, all these factors have, if anything, become more important. But what exactly has been their impact? Is it possible to speak of them as 'causes' of transnationalism?

Again, it is important not to oversimplify the way in which the process has unfolded. Take, for example, the rise of English as an international language. Though undoubtedly important, there is little evidence that its impact has been overwhelming. In the case of Al Qaeda, many of the middle managers – including figures like Khalid Sheikh Mohammed who planned the September 11 attacks – are multilingual and often speak not just two or three but five or six languages.[51] The group's lingua franca continues to be Arabic, which is the mother tongue of most of its leaders and the language of instruction in all the group's training camps. In fact, one of the reasons why the British authorities are less worried than their French or Spanish counterparts about the potential threat from 'returning jihadists', who went to train and fight in Iraq and are now going back to their countries of origin, is precisely because very few British grassroots jihadists (who are mostly of South Asian descent and whose first language is English) managed to find training camps in Iraq that were catering for non-Arabic speakers.[52] Language, in other words, remains a barrier to transnationalism, which (so far) the rise of English has only partially overcome.

Likewise, the idea that increased interconnectedness via information technology causes transnationalism overlooks not just barriers of language but also the uneven spread of these technologies. For instance, while Internet access is nearly universal now in Western Europe and North America, only 6 per cent of the population in the Arab world can use the new medium. Sageman is correct, of course, in pointing out that this figure fails to account for Internet usage in public places such as Internet cafes and libraries[53] but, even when this is factored in, there remains a significant disparity – at least for the time being – which cannot easily be explained away. As will be shown, the processes whereby information technologies facilitate transnationalism are more complicated than is suggested by the proposition which equates information technology with interconnectedness and transnationalism.

More generally, many of the arguments that are put forward in the literature confuse precipitating (or enabling) factors with causes. There can be no doubt that the three factors mentioned by Meyer, Boli and Thomas have contributed to interconnectedness and, thus, facilitated transnational exchange, but they do not explain what has caused transnationalism. Indeed, they could equally be cited as explanations for a surge in *inter*national – as opposed to *trans*national – activism: the rise of English, the spread of informational technology and the availability of cheap travel have also made it easier for terrorist organizations with a national or subnational focus to operate outside their countries of origins, activate diasporas and generate political and financial support in the international arena. The existence of new 'enablers', then, is insufficient as an explanation for the rise of transnational terrorist structures, and it is important, therefore, to look beyond the mechanics of interconnectedness and examine the underlying shifts in attitudes, ideology and identity that have underpinned and fuelled the transformation that can be witnessed in recent decades.

Global politics

A plausible explanation for the rise of transnationalism derives from changes in global politics and how they have been perceived. Arguably, the rise of transnationalism can be seen as an entirely rational – if not strategic – response to the widespread impression that major political actors have become increasingly interconnected, and that even local problems need to be addressed at the global level. In particular, state sovereignty is widely believed to be less absolute now than it used to be only two or three decades ago, and even strong, authoritarian governments are thought to be increasingly bound by international norms and regimes that regulate their behaviour.[54] Moreover, there is an increased awareness of international power relations, with external forces, both political and economic, thought to have major influence over domestic politics.[55] As a result, political activists – whether violent or peaceful – are less inclined to view domestic events as purely domestic in their origins and consequences, whilst international events are more likely to be seen as connected to the domestic arena. The idea of what constitutes the appropriate political unit through which grievances can be addressed is more muddled than just a few decades ago when the nation-state was still regarded as the ultimate arbiter of any conflict. For many political activists, then, responding to conflicts in a globally interconnected fashion simply reflects a perceived new reality.

The parallels between terrorist and non-terrorist transnational movements in this respect are striking. The social movement theorist Sidney Tarrow highlights the example of the austerity riots which occurred in many parts of the developing world in the mid-1980s.[56] Prompted by the structural adjustment programmes that had been imposed by international financial institutions such as the International Monetary Fund (IMF), trade union activists in countries as diverse as Argentina and Jamaica went to the streets, protesting against the measures that had to be implemented by national governments in order to qualify for financial aid. Although – as Tarrow points out – the 'repertoire of contention [was] astonishingly similar' across all the countries in which riots took place,[57] 'no transnational networks or solidarities appear in the accounts [of the demonstrations] and no unified organization grew out of the protests to coordinate an international movement'.[58] Rather than targeting the IMF, the protests were all directed against the national governments which, arguably, had little choice but to implement the conditions that had been dictated to them. It was only in the mid-1990s, when the discourse about globalization and global interconnectedness had become mainstream, that connections between the different protest movements emerged and attention gradually shifted from the national to the global context. This shift in perception then gave birth to the so-called 'anti-globalization' movement, which has become the focus of so many studies about transnationalism.[59]

When studying the evolution of transnational terrorism, it becomes clear that the shift from local to global occurred for similar reasons and at almost exactly the same time. Muslims from all over the world united in their fight against the Soviet occupation of Afghanistan in the 1980s, yet most of them initially returned to their home countries when victory had been achieved. In the early 1990s, they waged local struggles against what they saw as Muslim apostates ruling their countries. Though many of the campaigns in places like Egypt, Algeria, Jordan or Yemen were taking place concurrently – and despite the fact that many of the protagonists had forged close personal bonds during their time in Afghanistan – there was little coordination between them (see chapter 4).[60] Even Osama bin Laden seemed more preoccupied with the situation in his home country, Saudi Arabia, than with the state of the global community of believers, the *ummah*.[61] By the mid-1990s, however, the focus on local campaigns had given way to a renewed interest in external forces and the idea that there was a global conspiracy to suppress Islam. As bin Laden's deputy, Ayman al Zawahiri, explained:

> The struggle for the establishment of an Islamic state cannot be fought as a regional struggle. It has become . . . clear that the Alliance of Jews and Crusaders . . . will mobilize all its resources to defeat the jihad movement and prevent it from exercising power . . . In order to account for this *new reality*, we will have to prepare for a new battle which is not restricted to one particular region but which includes the near as well as the far enemy, the Alliance of Jews and Crusaders.[62] [emphasis added]

Noting the change in emphasis, the German scholar Guido Steinberg dates the emergence of Al Qaeda as a transnational movement to the year 1996 in which bin Laden first declared jihad against the United States.[63]

Looking at transnational terrorism within the broader context of transnational movements is instructive not just because most of the 'terrorism studies' literature fails to make this vital connection, but also because it highlights some of the opportunities and dilemmas common to all transnational movements – whether violent or not. For Tarrow, for example, transnationalism is a rational response to the 'new reality' of global interconnectedness, but it is rational also because it provides local movements with new ways to mobilize supporters and bring their campaigns to the attention of a wider audience.[64] Rather than running a local campaign against, say, the working conditions in a factory in India, 'global framing' allows activists to associate themselves with the broader (transnational) movement for 'global justice'. As a result, the cause will be adopted and promoted by people who would have shown scant interest in the lives of a few workers thousands of miles away had it not been for the narrative of global exploitation and injustice of which the campaign had suddenly become a part. Indeed, Tarrow believes that the local and the global have, in many cases, become inseparable, and that 'glocal' movements will increasingly represent the norm.[65] At the same time, he warns that attempts to globalize local struggles can also be a source of division, especially when not all the members of a movement share the global aspirations and/or rhetoric of their leaders.[66]

Tarrow's analysis is echoed by the evolution of transnational terrorist movements, especially Al Qaeda and its associates. As shown in the previous chapter, Al Qaeda has frequently been described as a 'franchise' organization, which unites – and provides a global frame for – a variety of local campaigns. There is plenty of anecdotal evidence that, prior to the September 11 attacks and the subsequent invasion of Afghanistan, local jihad leaders were competing for the attention of bin Laden, knowing that if they 'pitched' their respective campaigns as sufficiently global they would receive support from him. Bergen writes that, by 1998, 'something of a bin Laden cult' had taken hold, 'attract[ing] various militant Islamist groups into affiliate relationships with Al Qaeda'.[67] There can be no doubt that – in the course of doing so – some of the local campaigns ended up buying into the idea of global jihad. Others, however, became 'glocal' in that they started mixing local aims and objectives with 'global frames'. The Algerian Salafist Group for Preaching and Combat (GSPC), for example, adopted Al Qaeda in the Islamic Maghreb as its new name, which many experts interpreted as a step towards closer integration with the 'global jihad' promoted by bin Laden. Some of the older members of the organization immediately expressed their disagreement, arguing that the group should continue to focus on the struggle in Algeria and that the idea of creating a united Maghrebian caliphate was a pipe dream which would distract members from the more urgent task of toppling the secular government in Algiers. The resulting power struggle between 'nationalists' and 'transnationalists' has not just produced an ideological schism but effectively paralyzed the organization.[68]

Hybrid identities

A second factor that needs to be considered in explaining the rise of transnationalism is how profoundly globalization has challenged long-established forms of social and cultural identity. People's identities as part of particular communities and social classes had been stable for centuries until industrialization created radically new social and economic conditions which forced people to reassess and redefine traditional social customs and practices (see chapter 4). Urbanization raised these questions within the national context, but globalization extended the arena in which these processes are being played out from the national to the international level. As a result, identities have become ever more diverse, complex and contested, prompting – in the words of the political theorists Jonah Goldstein and Jeremy Rayner – 'a continuous process of self-examination [and, consequently], a continuous re-forming of who I am'.[69] Indeed, rather than being firmly rooted in one particular identity, people may come to regard themselves as members of multiple groups.[70] Some switch identities depending on their circumstances and the environment with which they are confronted. Yet others may adopt explicitly *trans*national identities in order to resolve the tensions they experience as a result of competing claims for their social and cultural allegiance. Transnational ideologies, in other words, are more attractive in the era of globalization than during earlier periods because they speak to people's perceptions of rootlessness, cultural and social displacement, and the consequent hybridization of their identities.

There are many aspects of, and processes associated with, globalization that could be said to be relevant in this respect, but what seem to be particularly significant are the medium- and long-term consequences of global migration. The International Organization of Migration has calculated that the overall number of migrants (that is, people permanently residing in countries other than their country of birth) worldwide has doubled since 1970: in 2005, it stood at around 200 million.[71] This figure, which represents nearly 3 per cent of the world's population, does not include the children of migrants who – by virtue of being born in the country in which their parents settled – are no longer considered migrants. Precise data on this second group, the 'second generation' descendants of migrants, is hard to come by, but it is safe to speculate that their number well exceeds that of the 'first generation'.[72] Perhaps for the first time in modern history, then, up to 10 per cent of the world's population – significantly more in the cities – have first- or second-hand experience of migration and have lived or grown up in countries and cultures that are different from their own or their parents'. Indeed, contemporary political debates about issues such as dual citizenship reflect the novelty of a situation for which there appears to be no precedent.[73]

How does this relate to terrorism? In 2002, the Dutch domestic intelligence service AIVD published a study of jihadist recruitment in the Netherlands which identified three types of 'personality' that could be found in extremist cells in Europe.[74] First were the so-called new immigrants, who had grown up in Middle Eastern and North African countries, and who came to Europe as students or refugees and had had no prior involvement with extremism before they arrived in the West. This applied to someone like Mohamed Atta, the Egyptian-born leader of the Hamburg cell that was responsible for the September 11 attacks, but it could also be said, for instance, of the perpetrators of the Glasgow attacks in July 2007 that were carried out by a group of graduates from the Middle East. The second group were second- or third-generation 'immigrants' whose parents or grandparents had settled in European countries as 'guest workers'. Most of the individuals in this group were citizens of European countries and spoke the language of their home country fluently. Finally, there was a small but growing number of converts who had embraced militant Islamism shortly after they had become Muslims.

Sageman, who conducted an extensive study of the profiles of Al Qaeda members, found that there was very little that would connect these groups in terms of quantifiable socioeconomic indicators.[75] Indeed, no researcher has yet been able to construct a single profile based on simple socio-economic indicators that would accurately describe the 'typical' jihadist.[76] However, what the three groups that were identified by the AIVD share is that – prior to joining a jihadist group – they had all experienced tensions in their personal lives or were faced with deep and sustained crises of identity which were resolved by embracing the transnational ideology of Al Qaeda. The 'new immigrants' felt alienated and isolated when they left their home countries, and extremist Islam not only provided them with new friends but also with a new identity and a place in the world. The children and grandchildren of immigrants frequently experience a tension between the traditional, cultural Islam of their parents and an unaccepting western society. Transnational extremism gave them an identity that allowed them to rebel against both. And the converts, by definition, had gone through a personal crisis that led them to adopt a new identity. Hence, with the exception of the converts, it becomes possible to establish a connection between aspects of the modern experience of global migration, a perceived conflict of identity, and the embracing of an extremist, transnational identity that seems to resolve this tension.[77]

It would, of course, be completely mistaken to conclude that migration produces terrorism. There is no evidence that terrorism *as such* is any more or less popular among migrants than it is among static populations. Rather, the point here is that a particular expression of terrorism – that is, terrorism with a transnational orientation – seems to have been underpinned by the modern condition of globalization. The French scholar Olivier Roy makes a similar point when he observes that, when dealing with Al Qaeda, 'we are facing not a diaspora but a truly de-territorialised population'.[78] Drawing on a large sample of Al Qaeda member profiles, he found that – in contrast to traditional diasporas – 'relations between [Al Qaeda] militants and their country of origin are weak or non-existent . . . Almost none of the militants fought in his own country, or in his family's country.'[79] Instead of appealing to any national or cultural allegiances with people's presumed countries of origin,

radical preachers and organizations in Europe were specifically targeting second-generation Muslims by 'playing on their
sense of being victims of racism, exclusion and loneliness in
the West' and offering a 'valorising substitute identity' which
transcended both western and traditional Muslim cultures.[80]
Despite its seemingly medieval rhetoric and social practices,
Roy concurs that Al Qaeda represents 'more a post-modern
phenomenon than a pre-modern one'.[81]

Virtual communities

A third factor, which has both driven and enabled the rise of
transnationalism, is the emergence of modern communication and information technologies. Over the past two decades,
the increase in the numbers of telephone, cell phone and
internet users has been unprecedented, and it would seem
natural for this to have some kind of effect on users' awareness of global issues.[82] But, as pointed out earlier, global
interconnectedness is not the same as transnationalism, nor
is it always clear how the former leads to the latter. What
matters is not merely the availability of information and the
possibility of new connections across national borders but,
rather, for what purposes they are being used. Indeed, what
many of the older studies on the rise of new information
technologies have failed to address is how, over the course
of two decades, global communication and interaction have
not just become dramatically faster, cheaper and (thus) more
extensive but how, as a result, these technologies have helped
to create virtual communities that are more susceptible to the
promotion of transnational orientations.

In the 1980s, there existed few channels through which
transnational ideas could have been conveyed. Newspapers,
radio and television were all targeting national audiences,
and they all strictly separated between domestic and international content. This began to change in the 1990s when

technological advances started to match transnational ideas with the transnational media through which they could be transported. First was the rise of satellite television, which – in the case of the Arab world – had the effect of reaffirming a sense of pan-Arab, pan-Muslim, identity,[83] and also provided new opportunities for the idea of a global conspiracy against Islam to be articulated in popular transnational forums (see pp. 53–4). Furthermore, the diffusion of cheap video-production technology made it possible for activists to provide visually powerful messages from places which had hitherto been considered unimportant or too difficult to access by the mainstream media. The conflict in Chechnya, for example, received such enormous attention among jihadists all over the world not least because the leader of the foreign fighters, the Saudi Ibn Khattab, insisted on filming every military operation. Realizing that modern technologies had made it possible to 'break the media siege', he argued that the mobilization of external support had become 'more important than rifles and guns'.[84] The video tapes which were smuggled out of Chechnya and disseminated all over the world on CDs played into the notion of a global war against Islam and are widely believed to have been critical in the radicalization of a second generation of jihadists in the Middle East and Europe.[85]

Only with the rise of the Internet, however, have transnational environments been able to function as communities. What made this new medium particularly attractive from the perspective of transnational groups was not just its low cost and that it allowed users to remain (more or less) anonymous[86] but, even more importantly, its global reach and the possibility of interaction. Only the Internet has made it possible for transnational organizations to overcome spatial constraints altogether and provide people with a sense of direct involvement in, and collective ownership of, events that are taking place thousands of miles away. In the case of Al Qaeda, one might argue that the very act of participating in jihadist web forums makes people experience the idea of being part of a global movement. As Sageman explains, the virtual community through which jihadists interact 'corresponds to the mythical [ummah] . . . which specifically rejects nationalism and fosters the global Salafi jihadi priority of fighting against the "far enemy" rather than the "near enemy"'.[87] In other words, the Internet both represents and powerfully projects the sense of community on which Al Qaeda's ideology rests.

Needless to say, the extent to which the Internet can function as a truly transnational community has limits. As pointed out earlier, access to the Internet is more widespread in certain countries than in others. Also, there continue to be language barriers, which means that virtual communities on the Internet are perhaps not quite as global as their participants think. Most importantly, while increasingly significant as a medium through which extremists communicate and generate a sense of community, the Internet rarely replaces real-world relationships altogether. In a recent study of Islamist militant recruitment in Europe which this author helped carry out,[88] none of the radicals or former radicals that were interviewed were radicalized or recruited solely on the Internet. Nor did any of the community leaders or law enforcement or intelligence officials that were spoken to believe that the Internet is likely ever to fully replace personal interaction. A university imam from North London summed it up as follows: 'Human contact is important because [recruitment] is all about who knows who. One guy knows a friend who knows a friend, and so on.'[89]

Real-world social relationships continue to be pivotal, and so do local concerns. Against this background, rather than eliminating people's local roots and substituting them with virtual communities, the principal function of the Internet seems to lie in embedding local issues within a transnational narrative. Some of the video clips that are currently available on jihadist sites, for example, appeal directly to second- and third-generation Muslims in Europe by combining the transnational narrative of 'the Muslim world under attack' with specifically European – sometimes even local – issues and experiences.[90] The aim is to suggest to young European Muslims that their sense of alienation and personal crisis can be attributed to the same forces that are causing the suffering of Muslims everywhere else, and that they are all part of one and the same struggle. In practice, then, the purpose of such videos is to weave together local and transnational perspectives, fostering 'glocal' rather than exclusively transnational attitudes, and it is in this respect that the Internet seems to play a particularly powerful role.

The aim of this chapter has been to examine how the diffusion of terrorist structures and their 'stretching' into transnational space has been facilitated by the dynamics and processes that are commonly identified as elements of globalization. As it turns out, the mechanics of causation are fairly straightforward. One might even argue that the evolution of terrorist group structures from 'old' to 'new' represents an entirely logical response to the new realities and opportunities that have arisen as a result of globalization.

The emergence of transnationalism, for example, mirrored changes in the international political system which suggested that the world had become more interconnected. It also constituted a response to global migration and the consequent hybridization of identities, which made an increasing number of people susceptible to transnational ideas and ideologies. This process was both driven and enabled by the rise of modern communication and information technologies which – especially with the Internet – provided new social environments through which transnational attitudes could be articulated. Terrorist groups 'stretching' into transnational space, in other words, took place against the background of a number of significant global changes which all favoured the bursting of the 'nationalist bubble' and one should not be surprised, therefore, that terrorist groups have adopted a similar outlook.

A similar argument could be made for the diffusion of terrorist structures. Information technology and the freer movement of people across borders have allowed terrorist groups to overcome spatial constraints and achieve more flexibility and efficiency in the running of their campaigns. Leaderships have taken advantage of new ways in which to communicate with sympathizers, whereas middle managers can draw on a wider pool of resources in planning and executing their operations. For the grassroots, advances in information technology in particular have provided new opportunities for getting involved. Again, therefore, the changes that have taken place represent a more or less consistent response to the way in which the process of globalization has unfolded.

However, if one accepts that the rise of transnational terror networks has echoed the processes associated with globalization, then answering the next question – namely, what explains the shift in terrorist aims and ideologies towards religion – may become more difficult. Indeed, one would expect globalization to promote more enlightened, more secular and more rational attitudes and ideologies, but what seems to have taken place is a rise in seemingly medieval ideas, which appears to contradict the notion of terrorism as a by-product of progressive change. This paradox will be at the centre of the following chapter.

CHAPTER FOUR

From Marx to Mohammed?
Religion and Terrorism

Some of the oldest known instances of terrorism can be attributed to groups or individuals claiming to act in the name of faith. As Bruce Hoffman points out, the Roman 'occupation' of Palestine was fought by the members of a small Jewish sect who called themselves Zealots and carried out 'dramatic acts of public violence', targeting Roman soldiers or their Jewish collaborators.[1] In India, a Hindu group known as Thugees terrorized travellers who would be strangled according to ritual and offered to the Goddess of destruction, Kali. The group was active from the seventh century and only ceased to exist in the middle of the nineteenth century.[2] And in today's Syria and Iran, an extremist splinter of the Muslim Ismaili sect – the so-called Assassins – killed scores of Christian crusaders beginning in the late eleventh century. Their violence 'was meant not only to vanquish the sect's Christian enemies but also to hasten the dawn of a new millennium'.[3]

Critics of the idea of new terrorism are completely right, therefore, to point out that there is nothing new about terrorism in the name of religion. It is equally clear, though, that there had been nearly no such terrorism for most of the twentieth century, and it is the reasons for this more recent 'return' of religiously inspired terrorism which this chapter hopes to explore. Based on the idea that terrorist groups always reflect broader ideological currents, it will be argued that the religious revival, the rise of radical religious politics and, by extension, religiously inspired terrorism are not contradictions, but inherent in the processes associated with late modernity and globalization. In the first section, it will be shown how recent religious revivals are related to late modernity. The second section will demonstrate why these revivals have become political and how some have turned to violence. This will be followed by an in-depth case study of the evolution of the rise of political Islam and Islamist terrorism, which aims to illustrate and substantiate the arguments put forward in the earlier sections.

Late modernity and the religious revival

As pointed out at the end of the previous chapter, the idea of modernity and the revival of seemingly archaic religious ideas are not an obvious match. How can globalization and modernity produce progress in one field and the apparent opposite in another? To understand how this apparent contradiction can be made sense of, it is essential to take a closer look at how globalization and late modernity have been perceived by people in the West and the developing world. First, though,it will be important to examine the historical trajectory of the debate about modernity and religion.

Religion and modernity

The notion that modernity and religion are opposed to each other is rooted in the Enlightenment, which began in the middle of the eighteenth century and whose central idea was for reason rather than tradition to be the guiding principle of all human endeavour. It inspired a number of important philosophical paradigms, including rationalism which demanded that all human behaviour and decision-making should be informed by the same logical processes from which insights in the natural sciences were derived. Another key concept, empiricism, postulated that all human knowledge should be gained from actual experience and systematic observation.[4] Not all Enlightenment thinkers agreed with each other, but they all believed in progress – progress through reason – and that 'The growth of knowledge [would enable] mankind to shape a future better than anything it has known in the past.'[5] The combination of reason and the belief in progress – together with a near-violent rejection of anything that could be construed as superstition – made the Enlightenment a uniquely powerful philosophical movement whose assumptions paved the way for modernity and continue to underlie, if not dominate, the western way of thinking.

Arguably, the whole idea of the Enlightenment was constructed in opposition to the way in which religious ideas and institutions were believed to have stifled progress and held back humanity in the past.[6] One only needs to read the French author Voltaire (who subscribed to the idea of a supreme being but rejected the Catholic church and much of its doctrine)[7] to understand quite how strongly the protagonists of the movement believed that people's potential would remain unfulfilled unless they freed themselves from the shackles of religious dogma. Conversely, they assumed that, if their ideas were allowed to spread, advances in technology, science and the resulting emancipation of society would make religion less plausible. The expectation was that knowledge and progress would lead to a decline in religious belief and practice: the more educated a society and the more it was governed by reason and rationality, the less it was necessary for people to look to religion and religious leaders for guidance.

For the first few decades following the end of the Second World War, the Enlightenment hypothesis seemed to be borne out by declining church attendance figures in Western Europe and the increasingly secular lifestyles of educated elites across the world.[8] By the mid-1970s, however, sociologists and anthropologists were surprised to find that the seemingly unstoppable advance of secularism had come to a halt. Instead, conservative religious groups were springing up on all continents and in all cultures. The rise of the evangelical movement in the United States, Europe and parts of Latin America was echoed by the emergence of Hindu nationalism in India, the Islamic revival in the Middle East and the resurgence of orthodox Judaism in Israel and among diaspora Jews. Indeed, it did not take long until the various religious revivals came to be reflected in politics. The French Middle East expert Gilles Kepel singles out the second half of the 1970s as a turning point: in 1977, strong gains for the religious parties ended nearly thirty years of Labour party rule in Israel; in 1978, the election of Karol Wojtyla as Pope John Paul II signalled the return to a more traditionalist interpretation of Catholic doctrine; and in 1979, Ayatollah Khomeini's movement expelled the Shah from Tehran and established the Islamic Republic of Iran.[9]

Clearly, the Enlightenment hypothesis had failed to predict that people even in highly advanced societies could turn their back on progress and reason and revert to religious practices which many liberal minds considered anachronistic. How, then, could the sudden reversal be explained? In the early 1990s, many scholars began to argue that the two seemingly contradictory phenomena – late modernity and the religious revival – were in fact connected. Among the first to address the conundrum, Kepel argued that the return to religion was a reaction to the 'worldwide discrediting of modernism'.[10] He noted that, 'wherever [religious revivalism] appears, it sets itself up against a "crisis" in society, claiming to have identified the underlying causes of that crisis beyond the economic, political or cultural symptoms through which it is manifested'.[11] Writing at almost exactly the same time, the academic Frank Lechner went even further, arguing that revivalist movements represented a form of resistance against not just modernity but, more specifically, the forces of globalization. In his view, the emergence of such groups was 'one effort among others to preserve or achieve a certain cultural authenticity in the face of a greedy, universalizing global culture'.[12]

Though somewhat more sophisticated than the Enlightenment hypothesis, these arguments ignored many of the subtleties which characterized the movements they sought to describe. Most significantly, they looked at the religious revival as if it represented a 'return to tradition', whereas in reality it was an entirely novel expression of religiosity that often had no precedent in a particular country's religious history. Though using the language of religion, there was nothing 'culturally authentic' about, say, the Islamic Salafi movement, which had been virtually unknown outside of Saudi Arabia prior to the religious revival of the 1970s, nor did evangelical Christians have any tradition to go back to in historically Catholic countries like Brazil. It was misleading, therefore, to view the religious revival in terms of a confrontation between tradition and modernity.

Only in the mid-1990s did scholars manage to reconcile the religious revival with modernity. The American futurologist John Naisbitt conceived the notion of the 'global paradox', observing that, as globalization unfolds, people have a tendency to revert to more 'tribal' concerns, such as ethnicity, language and religion.[13] The political scientist Benjamin Barber popularized the terms 'jihad' and 'McWorld' as metaphors for the dialectic forces that marked the late modern experience. His explanation is worth quoting at length:

> What I have called forces of Jihad may . . . appear to be directly adversarial to the forces of McWorld. Yet Jihad stands not so much in stark opposition as in subtle counterpoint to McWorld and is itself a dialectical response to modernity whose features both reflect and reinforce the modern world's virtues and vices – Jihad *via* McWorld rather than Jihad *versus* McWorld . . .

Modernity precedes and thus sponsors and conditions its critics. And though those critics, on the way to combating the modern, may try to resuscitate ancient usages and classical norms, such usages and norms – ethnicity, fundamentalist religion, nationalism, and culture for example – are themselves at least in part inventions of the agitated modern mind. Jihad is not only McWorld's adversary, it is its child.[14] [original emphasis]

Though Barber had mostly nationalism in mind and was referring to religious movements only in passing,[15] his central idea – namely that 'fundamentalist' movements are products of modernity rather than the past – still provides the most compelling prism through which to interpret the religious revival that began in the late 1970s. At the same time, his concept of 'jihad *via* McWorld' left the central question unanswered. What is it about late modernity that makes people want to embrace 'fundamentalist' religious movements? How exactly does exposure to late modernity lead to a revival in religiosity?

Late modernity and insecurity

The key to unpacking the complex relationship between 'Jihad' and 'McWorld' lies in understanding how late modernity has not just made societies freer and more productive but how, in so doing, it has simultaneously produced more anxiety. When looking at western countries, one can easily identify a whole range of uniquely late modern developments that have contributed to this widespread sense of insecurity. Take, for example, the use of technology and how it has challenged people's sense of control over their own destiny. As the American journalist George Will explains, late modernity has '[multiplied] . . . dependencies on things utterly mysterious to those who are dependent – things such as semiconductors, which control the functioning of almost everything from cell phones to computers to cars'.[16] Whenever such complex systems fail, people realize that their late modern existence relies on institutions and processes they do not know or understand and whose workings they cannot influence. In fact, many have come to understand that, with many such systems being interdependent, it takes the failure of just one system – say, electricity or computers – in order for its effects to 'cascade down' and affect other vital systems.[17] Hence, while modern western societies may have attained a degree of sophistication that is unparalleled in human history, it is precisely their sophistication that has made them vulnerable. Technical and scientific progress has not necessarily led to more control but, on the contrary, it has produced an all-pervasive sense of fragility.[18]

A second factor that needs to be considered is the massive economic and social changes that western societies have undergone in the decades following the Second World War. As early as 1986, the German sociologist Ulrich Beck pointed out that, with the rise of structural unemployment, part-time work and the idea of job mobility, many of the certainties that had marked employment in the modern area had ceased to exist. These changes, he argued, had been accompanied by equally dramatic transformations in the social sphere, especially new generational values and gender equality.[19] And indeed, people in western societies get married later, have fewer children and are divorced more frequently.[20] The traditional constants of marriage, family and lifetime employment, which brought stability to life in the modern era, no longer seem to be reliable guides for late modern biographies. There can be no doubt that late modernity has introduced more flexibility and choice – people are less constrained by family, neighbourhood, culture and social convention – but this has also created new demands. Life in the late modern era may be filled with opportunities, yet the overabundance of opportunity also seems to have created uncertainty and confusion.

More recently, globalization has added a further dimension to the widespread sense of insecurity experienced by western societies. In the previous chapter, it was shown how global migration has created hybrid identities, especially among the second- and third-generation descendants of immigrants, and how this has contributed to the attractiveness of transnational identities and ideologies. The impact of global migration, however, has not been restricted to the immigrants them-selves. Being confronted with the cultural, ethnic and religious 'other', whether in the form of immigrants or other foreign influences, has compelled indigenous populations to question their own sense of identity. The academic John Tomlinson cites the example of Mexican labourers who, upon moving to the United States, 'were pressed to . . . adopt a particular form of . . . identity as a member of a collective or "community"',[21] and – in turn – made Americans think harder about their own identity. The same process, albeit on a larger scale, can be observed in Western Europe. The influx of foreign labour, which began in the late 1950s and 1960s, turned monocultural into multicultural societies and, in doing so, has raised uncom-fortable questions about what it actually means to be British, German or French. Globalization and late modernity, then, have not just spread a generalized sense of uncertainty and instability but challenged the very idea of national identity.[22]

In developing countries, the tension between jihad and 'McWorld' results not from the transition between modernity and late modernity but, rather, from the unsettling clashes that occur between the pre-modern, modern, and late modern elements that co-exist in many of these societies. The geo-graphical space in which such clashes are played out are the cities whose populations have multiplied in the course of the post-war demographic explosion and the resulting mass migration from the countryside, which the sociologist Saskia Sassen pointedly described as 'people on the run'.[23] Such mega-cities contain the 'new arrivals' from the countryside; the recently settled lower and middle classes who occupy (often badly paid) jobs in trade, services and the industrial sector; and the (western) educated elites whose values, attitudes and lifestyles often resemble those of their late modern counterparts in the developed world.

While each of these groups would have plenty of reason to feel anxious on their own, it is the interaction between them that has made their experience particularly intense. The lower and middle classes, for example, have long been frustrated about their lack of economic progress and access to higher social strata, especially in former colonies where the struggle for independence was accompanied by the hope for more justice and equity. What has caused them anxiety are the 'recent arrivals' who are competing against them for income, jobs and, more generally, a place in society. As a result, rather than moving up the social ladder, the lower and middle classes feel that they need to fight in order to keep what little they have got. For the 'recent arrivals', the challenge is both economic and social. Not only do they need to make ends meet, they also have to learn to cope in unsettling social environments with unfamiliar customs and practices. For instance, the Pakistan-born political scientist Mustapha Pasha points out that, 'removed from established patterns of rural life, the vast majority of Muslim youth who now inhabit the congested cities [in South Asia and the Arab world] confront unexpected . . . encounters with the opposite sex'.[24] Tossed into a 'new social universe' in which they lack orientation and cultural points of reference,[25] many of the 'recent arrivals' are certain to go through periods of tension and uncertainty.

As in the developed world, globalization has added to the widespread sense of insecurity. The academic Jamal Nassar shows that, while globalization may have shrunk distances, it has simultaneously raised expectations, especially in the developing world where, thanks to the expansion of foreign tourism, returning labour migrants and satellite television, the dispossessed and the poor have been educated about '[their] own poverty and dispossession versus the rising wealth and power of the few'.[26] It may well be true that economic globalization has benefited millions, but these benefits have not 'migrated' as fast as people's expectations,[27] nor have they reached all the developing countries to the same extent. In 2005, a high-level working group of political economists, which convened at the International Summit on Democracy, Terrorism and Security in Madrid, concluded that some countries' successful integration into the world economy had been mirrored by

> the growth of 'weak globalisers' who become less competitive, whose populations have failing or stagnant incomes, and – as a result – experience growing unemployment, political tension, and religious fundamentalism. A number of African and Muslim countries have steadily 'de-globalised' over the last 25 years. The general effects are an increase in inequalities and social polarisation.[28]

Indeed, it is often overlooked that the same process of stratification has occurred *within* as well as between developing societies, and that, in many countries, the success of some has caused others to feel left behind. As the Indian journalist Anand Giridharadas points out:

> Societies are not monolithic blocks that go global all at once. Social change has early and late adopters, and the choices of the timely alter the options among which the tardy must subsequently choose. And so a defining fact about globalization may be that it has freed untold millions from inherited destinies, even as it makes others feel as though their control over fate is slipping away.[29]

Those societies – or segments within societies – that have so far failed to take advantage of any economic benefits may experience globalization as a threat. From their perspective, not only does globalization seem to fail to deliver on the promise of prosperity, it is sometimes viewed as a pretext for the imposition of alien values and culture. Globalization, therefore, has accentuated the conflict between the pre-modern, modern and late modern sections of developing societies and, thus, contributed to the general sense of instability which has marked many of these countries' recent history.

Despite a similar analysis of the problem, much of the literature in the 1990s focused almost exclusively on the resurgence of ethno-nationalist identities. Barber himself concluded – somewhat confusingly – that 'the language most commonly used to address the ends of the reinvented and self-described tribes waging Jihad . . . remains the language of nationalism'.[30] This may have been the obvious conclusion to draw at the time, given the numerous instances of war, ethnic cleansing and even genocide that followed the break-ups of Yugoslavia and the Soviet Union. In reality, though, nationalism was just one of several ways in which people could express their desire for certainty in an uncertain world. An equally powerful source was religion, yet Barber and many of his colleagues had lost the courage of their convictions: having correctly identified the dialectics of late modernity and the resurgence of identity which it had produced, they pushed religion to the margins, believing that it was of secondary importance.

In many ways, of course, religion was the more obvious source of identity in a rapidly changing global environment. Where people believed that they had lost control over their destiny, religion offered a sense of direction and guidance. Where people were confused and overwhelmed by new choices and unfamiliar social environments, religion brought clarity and purpose. And where people felt threatened by instability, religion offered a way of making peace with themselves and the seemingly chaotic world around them. In short, religion provided meaning, direction and a sense of belonging in a world which appeared to have lost its way.

The two revivals – religious and nationalist – not only shared the same roots, they also seem to have followed similar trajectories. Although their violent manifestations often became obvious only in the 1990s, they can both be traced back to the 1970s and 1980s.[31] There was one important difference, of course. Nationalism was political by definition, whereas religion and the religious revival were spiritual in the first and political only in the second instance. It may have been reasonable to assume, therefore, that the religious revival was less likely than the nationalist resurgence to 'tip over' into political violence. Yet it did, and in the following section it will be explained how and why this happened.

Religion, politics and violence

Some of the most widely held views about religiously motivated terrorism are wrong. One of the most popular beliefs is that religiously motivated violence is somehow beyond reason and that it cannot possibly be explained with reference to rational calculation. Even otherwise reasonable and respected scholars such as Herfried Münkler argue that the new, religiously motivated terrorism is different from previous manifestations of the phenomenon because it has no real-world constituency to which the terrorists would be accountable for their actions.[32] Likewise, the American political psychologist Jerrold Post maintains that none of the rules that were developed for 'ordinary' terrorists apply to religiously motivated terrorists because they 'are not constrained by their audience on earth'.[33] This may well be true for the most extreme, cult-like groups, such as the Japanese Aum Shinrikyo, whose attack on the Tokyo Underground in 1995 was intended to hasten the apocalypse. But few observers any

longer doubt that organizations like Al Qaeda have a strategy. Indeed, anyone who has read some of the recent online
exchanges between Osama bin Laden's deputy, Ayman al
Zawahiri, and his critics will be aware that Al Qaeda's leadership is highly conscious not just of religious doctrine but the
views and opinions of its followers and the Arab street more
generally (see chapter 5).[34]

Equally misguided is the attempt to separate 'religious' from
'political' terrorism as if the two categories were mutually
exclusive. If the only goal is to bring about Armageddon – as
in the case of Aum Shinrikyo – the classification of a group as
'political' may indeed be questionable. But if the objective is
to change or transform societies by introducing aspects of religious law, creating a theocracy or even a caliphate – however
misguided or unrealistic these ideas may be – the political
nature of the terrorist campaign can no longer be in doubt.
In fact, as shown in chapter 2, the strict separation between
religiously and politically motivated terrorism often hinders a
greater understanding of individual groups. Not only do many
religiously inspired groups, such as Hamas and Hezbollah,
have multiple – that is, religious and ethnic-nationalist –
agendas, the degree to which they are influenced by religious
doctrine can differ significantly: Hamas is not Al Qaeda, nor
is Al Qaeda the same as Aum Shinrikyo. What all politically
motivated terrorist groups – whether religiously or otherwise
inspired – share is that their political programmes are violent
expressions of ideological currents which are located on the
radical fringes of mainstream society. In other words, they
reflect broader political and/or social trends, and it is to these
that their ideological origins must be traced.

In explaining how some of the religious revivals that were
described in the previous section turned into religiously
motivated terrorism, one needs to distinguish between two
processes. First, it is necessary to understand the conditions

that have pushed religious movements into the political sphere. Why were the followers of the religious revival no longer content to pursue their faith in private? What explains their sudden interest in articulating views about society and how it ought to be organized? Having understood what caused the politicization of religious movements, one then needs to look at how they turned to violence. Why did they abandon their strategy of peaceful opposition? How did they mobilize their followers?

As will be shown, the first development – that is, the politicization of religion – can only be understood with reference to the particular conditions of late modernity and globalization, whereas the second process – that of turning to violence – is more generic and draws on insights gained about the dynamics of violent radicalization and mobilization more generally. In fact, it is the interplay between specific conditions and the more generic processes of violent radicalization and mobilization that best explains how the religious revival and the rise of religiously inspired violence have manifested themselves.

Turning to politics

First, then, what are the conditions that have pushed the religious revival into the political sphere? Two explanations stand out. The first argues that all forms of secular governance had failed, especially in the developing world, and that religion was the one culturally authentic alternative.[35] During the Cold War, most of the so-called Third World countries had to align themselves with one of the two superpowers, yet neither communism nor capitalism provided the kinds of economic and social improvements which many people had hoped for, particularly in countries which had achieved independence only in the post-war period. On the contrary, secular nationalism – be it of the communist or the capitalist variety – was experienced as corrupt, oppressive and highly inefficient. Paradoxically, then, the same secular ideologies that had mobilized the masses in the name of national liberation when under colonial rule came to be seen as forms of locally administered colonialism – a cunning way of exporting imperialist ideas 'from the western world, where [they] first emerged, to the rest of the world'.[36] Against this background, religiously inspired government was perceived not only as a plausible alternative but, even more importantly, as the return to a culturally authentic way of life – even if the particular variety of religion that emerged as a result of the religious revival was sometimes far from authentic.[37]

This process, of course, did not unfold everywhere. While almost every society that has been touched by modernity has experienced some form of religious revival, the politicization of new religious movements happened in some parts of the world (especially the United States, parts of Africa, Israel, the Muslim world and India) but not in others (for example, Europe, Latin America and large parts of Asia). It is beyond the scope of this book to consider each of these places in detail, but the 'failure of secularism' hypothesis may help to explain at least some of the regional variation. In the Muslim world and India, for example, religiously inspired political ideologies were well positioned to offer a clear and tangible alternative to what many people regarded as the secular, neo-colonialist status quo. This was because the colonial experience had been relatively recent and the language of the religious revival – Islam and Hindu nationalism respectively – provided a marker of cultural distinctiveness from the West. In Latin America, on the other hand, secularism was no longer bound up with colonialism in the public mind because most countries had been independent for more than a century. Also, the religious revival promoted an entirely novel, more distinctly western version of Christianity (Protestantism) at the expense of the more traditional, historically rooted one (Catholicism).

As a consequence, not only was there no demand for non-secular ideologies, it was hard to convey the religious revival as culturally authentic.

A second explanation focuses on the widening gap between religious lifestyles and the social realities of late modernity. The movements which emerged as a result of the religious revival are often described as 'fundamentalist'[38] because they distinguish themselves from the rest of society in dress, customs and conduct. They are committed to conservative values, interpret holy texts as literally as possible, and – more often than not – hope to imitate an idealized past in which they believe perfect conditions for a sacred life existed. Modern and late modern societies have made it increasingly difficult for such 'fundamentalists' to live their lives in accordance with their ideas. Most modern societies grant religious freedom and protect individuals' right to exercise their faith. But they also conceive of religion as a private affair, with the result that – to varying degrees – religious expression has been excluded from the public arena. In the words of the American constitutional scholar John Garvey, modern societies have enforced a 'clean separation: religion is a private affair; the public sphere is secular'.[39] Consequently, 'fundamentalists' have found themselves in social and political environments which they increasingly regarded as alien to their way of life. Globalization, which has imported foreign influences and increasingly liberal lifestyles, only added to the perception that people's religious identities were under threat and – more generally – that it had become impossible to reconcile religious principles with life in modern, secular societies.

Faced with seemingly hostile societies, fundamentalists had to make a choice. One option was to withdraw and separate from mainstream society. In the United States, Christian evangelicals set up compounds in the sparsely populated western states, established evangelical universities and colleges, and even took their children out of state schools so they could be taught at home. The purpose was to isolate and protect themselves from modern life which was believed to contaminate the purity of the faith. In the words of the academic Michael Apple, 'This "cocooning" is not just about seeking an escape from the problems of the city (a metaphor for danger and heterogeneity). It is a rejection of the entire *idea* of the city. Cultural and intellectual diversity, complexity, ambiguity, uncertainty and proximity to the Other – all these are to be shunned'[40] [original emphasis].

A similar approach – albeit far more extreme – was practised by a group of Islamists in Egypt in the 1970s who became known as Takfir wal-Hijra. Confronted with a society which they believed was morally corrupt, their leader, Shukri Mustafa, decided to excommunicate all of Egyptian society and then withdraw from 'godless society'. Together with his followers, he set up camps in Upper Egypt where the group prepared for their triumphant return after the inevitable breakdown of the existing order.[41]

The other option consisted of the exact opposite: instead of withdrawing from society, some fundamentalists concluded that the public space had to be made safe for religion again. In their view, it was no longer sufficient for the state to protect people's right to exercise their religious freedom in private when the whole society had, in essence, become a vast conspiracy to prevent believers from being good Muslims/ Christians/Jews and so on. All true believers had to be called upon to cross the 'secular line' and engage in politics so that the societal order would, once again, come to reflect the religious ideas and principles according to which life ought to be organized.[42] Religion and religious identity thus turned into political activism and, for some, into a radical political project, which – rather than merely safeguarding the right of believers to freely practise their religion and propagate their faith – advocated the transformation of all society according to religious principles. Ultimately, of course, this meant imposing religiously inspired principles and tenets on those who were exercising their right to practise a different faith or no faith at all.

Turning to violence

What, then, explains how radical and religiously inspired movements have turned to violence? As mentioned above, the process of violent radicalization draws on mechanisms that are generic to any movement, regardless of its particular ideological orientation. Moreover, in looking at this process, it is important to separate strategic choices from the conditions that have shaped them. Indeed, the decision to adopt violent means can be seen as a calculated, strategic choice, resulting from a deep sense of frustration about the ineffectiveness of peaceful means. As Leonard Weinberg demonstrated, the vast majority of terrorist groups did not start out with the intention of employing violent means, but chose to adopt violence when their political ambitions had failed.[43] They came to the realization that authoritarian regimes in particular are skilful manipulators of political, religious and ethnic divides, and that even the most despotic governments appear to generate enough support and acquiescence for most challenges to their power to remain ineffective. Sensing that their message was 'not getting through', they concluded that only the use of truly extraordinary means could guarantee interest and publicity, destabilize the regime, frighten the ruling classes or incite those who were considered too timid to take up arms to join the movement. It is this belief in the transformative power of symbolic violence – often referred to as the 'propaganda of the deed' – which lies at the heart of any strategy of terrorism.[44]

Even the most calculated decision, however, does not occur in a political vacuum. As many studies have shown, the choice of violence is frequently preceded by so-called triggers[45] which accelerate the process whereby radical movements opt for violence. One such trigger can be harsh government repression. Faced with a challenge to their authority, governments may decide to suppress non-violent opposition movements by restricting their ability to assemble and organize, by banning their associations and newspapers, or even by arresting, interning, torturing and killing their representatives. If the governments' repression is not efficient, ruthless and total, the likely outcome is that the surviving activists become more extreme. Having convinced themselves that there is no longer any value in seeking compromise within the present system, they may conclude that there is no choice but to engage in a violent confrontation.[46]

A second type of trigger is so-called 'traumatic' events which generate shock and a sense of moral outrage among the movement's activists and supporters.[47] These events take different forms and may include the invasion of a country, the killing of an important political or spiritual leader, or even the passing of a particular law. What makes such events 'traumatic' is the movement's deep sense of emotional empathy with those involved or potentially affected – even if they are thousands of miles away – and the consequent impression that urgent action is necessary in order to avert an existential crisis and/ or take the struggle forward. Traumatic events, therefore, not only translate feelings of hurt and humiliation – often experienced not directly but 'by proxy'[48] – into anger and the sudden determination to 'do something', but generate an overwhelming desire and perceived need to step up the campaign.[49]

Triggers are not unique to religiously inspired movements, but religiously motivated radicals may experience them in particularly intense ways. When faced with harsh government repression, for example, religious movements are more likely to perceive confrontations as existential. As the American scholar Jessica Stern argues, religion is the 'ideal mobilization tool' because 'the Other is often inherent' and sharp distinctions between the in-group and the out-group – between believers and unbelievers, the saved and the condemned, for example – are more easily drawn.[50] The same is true for traumatic events, which may be regarded as preordained and whose significance is more likely to be exaggerated. Indeed, one of the most distinguished scholars of religious violence, Mark Juergensmeyer, points out that the language and imagery of religion – the idea of 'cosmic' wars, the confrontation between 'good' and 'evil', and so on – tends to amplify the impact of events and thus contributes to the ferocity with which religiously inspired movements are likely to respond.[51] Rather than acting as a barrier against the use of violence, religion thus serves as ideological fuel that hastens the decision to adopt violent means.

Once a movement has 'tipped over' into violence, the shape, size and potency of the terrorist campaign will be determined by how well a group can be mobilized. Again, the basic elements of this process are similar for any movement regardless of motivation. Effective mobilization requires strong ('charismatic') leadership; a clear idea of what the group aims to achieve and how this can be accomplished (strategic direction); some technical skills and expertise; and – not least – a certain amount of financial and other material resources. The only aspect in which religiously motivated groups differ from this template is that they require acts of violence to be justified in theological terms. After all, in most religions, many of the activities that may be involved in a terrorist campaign – for instance, killing people and suicide – are heavily regulated or strictly forbidden. As a result, religiously inspired groups always have an element of religious authority through which a compelling rationale for how particular acts are to be reconciled with scripture can be provided.[52]

An excellent illustration of how this process plays out in practice is the Army of God, a little-known American Christian group that was responsible for hundreds of attacks on abortion clinics, including seven assassinations, mostly of doctors and medical staff in the 1990s.[53] The group is a product of the evangelical revival in the United States, and its leading activists had been on the fringes of the evangelical Right for years prior to their launching of the group. While the abortion issue has been the Army of God's principal focus, its agenda has always gone beyond this single issue. The group's key document – titled *When Life Hurts, We Can Help* – makes clear that its ideologists believe the 'rapid decline of western thought and culture' to be the root cause of abortion and other perceived ills of contemporary American society.[54] In an interview, the Reverend Michael Bray – a Lutheran minister who is often described as the group's religious authority[55] – told Juergensmeyer that he saw 'American society in a state of utter depravity, over which its elected officials presided with an almost satanic disregard for truth and human life'.[56] His vision, according to Juergensmeyer, was 'the establishment of a new moral order in America, one based on biblical law and a spiritual, rather than a secular, social compact'.[57] Hence, while the abortion issue was the group's immediate priority, the transformation of American society was the wider, underlying aim which informed members' attitudes and shaped their view of the world.

Activists associated with the group had been involved in 'direct action' against abortion clinics for years, but the killing of medical staff only began in 1993. Juergensmeyer believes that the group's violent turn was related to Bill Clinton's presidential election victory in 1992 and the perception that, more than ever, the federal government was 'undermining individual freedoms and moral values', which made life for Christians in a secular society impossible.[58] Another explanation is the decline of Operation Rescue, a grassroots initiative of anti-abortion activists who were staging sit-ins at abortion clinics, chaining themselves to doctors' cars and harassing people who wanted to enter the premises. Operation Rescue was so successful that the American Congress had to make the blocking of access to medical clinics a criminal offence. Following the passing of the law, the number of incidents at abortion clinics fell rapidly and Operation Rescue gradually dissolved.[59] For those who came to be involved in the Army of God, the combination of a new, liberal and outspokenly pro-choice government, together with the closing of all 'legitimate' avenues for protest, may well have amounted to a perceived crisis – or trigger – in which the killing of people became a justified and, indeed, necessary means to stop what members regarded as the Great Holocaust.[60]

The Army of God had virtually no financial resources at its disposal, nor were its members particularly skilled or experienced in running campaigns of violence. The rise of the Internet made it possible for the group to gain some notoriety and claim that it operated according to the principles of 'leaderless resistance'. It published a 136-page manual which contains instructions on everything from carrying out arson to launching chemical and biological attacks. One of the group's leading activists (who himself claims that the Army of God is a myth invented by the federal authorities)[61] maintains a web site – the so-called *Nuremberg Files* – with the names and personal details of doctors who are performing abortions. Yet, while some of the smaller attacks may indeed have been carried out by 'leaderless resisters' who were inspired by what they found on the Internet, all the killings have been attributed to a tightly knit group of no more than fifty core activists who, until 2001, were meeting annually at the so-called White Rose Banquet (hosted by Bray).[62] Although the Army of God has some sympathizers among the evangelical movement, the group's violent tactics have divided its core constituency and led to strong condemnations from more mainstream figures. Together with the absence of a powerful 'mobilizer' – for example, a state – this has meant that the Army of God's appeal has remained limited.

If anything, the case of the Army of God illustrates that a multitude of processes are at work in effecting the shift from religious revival to religiously inspired terrorism. Late modernity and globalization have provided the 'breeding grounds' for the politicization of religious movements, but whether or not a 'violent turn' occurs depends on a number of additional factors, including movements' strategic choices, the presence of triggers and, not least, the degree to which grievances, conditions and external audiences can be mobilized effectively. In the following section, this 'toolbox' will be used to explore the origins and rise of what is undoubtedly the most important contemporary manifestation of religiously inspired terrorism.

Political Islam and Islamist terrorism

Although religiously motivated terrorism can be found in all faiths and cultures, this section is devoted exclusively to (Sunni) political Islam and Islamist terrorism. More than, say, Christian or Jewish fundamentalism, the rise of political Islam and the emergence of Islamist terrorism have defined the current age. Those who claim to act in the name of Islam have killed more people in the last two decades than any other branch of religiously inspired terrorism. This includes the most devastating terrorist attack of all time, Al Qaeda's attacks against the United States on 11 September 2001, which killed as many people in one day than had died in thirty years of conflict in Northern Ireland. Conversely, countries such as Afghanistan and Iraq have been invaded in order to halt the spread of Islamist terrorism, and much of international politics – especially in relation to the Muslim world – is seen through the prism of what hinders or helps the fight against it. It is not prejudice, therefore, that has determined the choice of subject but, rather, a careful reflection of how the phenomenon of religiously inspired terrorism is currently being expressed.

Needless to say, this brief account cannot hope to match the works of academics who have dedicated their entire lives to researching the subject. Nor does it intend to add anything to their scholarship. Instead, the aim is to draw on their findings and see how they relate to what has been said about the shift from religion to politics and religiously inspired terrorism. In particular, the questions to be explored in the following are: why did the religious revival in (Sunni) Islam become political, and how did political Islam (Islamism) produce its violent 'offspring'?

The rise of political Islam

It is difficult to define a starting point for political Islam, but it seems clear that, for most of its founding fathers, it was the encounter with western modernity in the late colonial period which pushed their hitherto private religiosity into the political sphere. Arguably, its most important representatives in the first half of the twentieth century were Hassan al-Banna, who founded the Egyptian Muslim Brotherhood, and Mawlana Mawdudi, who established a similar group, the Jamaat-e-Islami, in Pakistan.[63] Though separated by thousands of miles, they interpreted the state of their respective countries in very similar ways. According to John Esposito, an American scholar of Islam, 'Both placed primary blame for the ills of their society and the decline of the Muslim world upon European imperialism and westernized Muslim elites. Like revivalists of old, they initially called for moral and social reform but soon also became embroiled in political activism and opposition.'[64]

In Egypt, the confrontation between the Muslim Brotherhood and the government quickly turned violent. The 1950s and 1960s saw several waves of repression during which the ideological 'godfather' of Islamist militancy,[65] Sayyid Qutb, was incarcerated and executed. Qutb's writings were significant because they turned the ideas of al-Banna and Mawdudi into a revolutionary ideology, which postulated that all of Egyptian society lived in an age of ignorance (*jahiliya*) and that the violent overthrow of the country's regime – which he defined as jihad – in order to establish a truly Islamic state (governed by shariah law) was not just legitimate but an individual obligation for every righteous believer. According to Esposito:

> For Qutb, jihad, as armed struggle in the defense [sic] of Islam against the injustice and oppression of anti-Islamic governments and the neo-colonialism of the West and the East . . . was incumbent on all Muslims. Those who refused to participate were to be counted among the enemies of God and should be excommunicated or declared unbelievers, or *takfir*, and fought and killed along with the other enemies of God.[66]

To this day, Qutb's ideas provide the intellectual underpinning for the campaigns of Islamist terrorists all over the world.[67]

The ideological development of radical Islam preceded its rise as a popular mass movement by several decades. At the time of Qutb's imprisonment, most countries in the Arab world had just won independence from their former colonial masters, often in hard-fought struggles for national liberation. Initially, people in countries like Algeria, Tunisia and Morocco were optimistic about the future, believing that the end of imperialism would bring new freedoms and a rise in economic prosperity. In Egypt, President Gamal Abdel Nasser had electrified much of the Arab world with his idea of pan-Arabism, a form of secular nationalism that was regarded as a confident, if not aggressive, expression of Arab independence (so much so that some European countries regarded him as a threat). In Nasser's Egypt, as in most other Muslim countries that were allied with the Soviet Union, Islam had been pushed to the margins and no longer played any significant role in the public sphere. Likewise, in those countries that were associated with the West, Islamic 'clergy' were reduced to the role of 'helping governments by issuing fatwas (religious rulings) and endorsing their state policies'.[68]

Islam had been thoroughly secularized, but it had not been eliminated. Faith institutions of various kinds – ranging from mosques and prayer halls to mystic brotherhoods and educational establishments – still formed the core of civil society in most Muslim countries.[69] And it was through these institutions and networks that popular opposition movements came to be mobilized when the experiment with Arab nationalism fell to pieces. The turning point, which dramatically reversed the fortunes of secular nationalism, was the Six-Day War in 1967, when Israel inflicted a humiliating defeat on the combined armies of Syria, Egypt and Jordan. It exposed the shallowness of Nasser's rhetoric, as well as the fragility of the post-independence settlement more generally, and prompted a period of deep reflection during which Arab societies reconsidered fundamental questions about their character and identity. A leader of the Tunisian Islamist movement who had previously been a supporter of Nasser remembers thinking that 'Islamic civilization was showing all the symptoms of the diseases that affected western civilization. Modernisation had not only given us western science and technology, but also its maladies.'[70] He, like many others, eventually concluded that the essence of Arab culture lay not in pan-Arab nationalism but Islam: 'Arabism had no other cultural identity except the Muslim one.'[71]

Throughout most of the 1970s, the violent struggles in the Muslim world continued to be led by nationalist and/

or socialist movements such as the Palestinian Liberation Organization (PLO). With the exception of the Egyptian Muslim Brotherhood, political Islam had not yet been mobilized. This changed towards the end of the decade. Undoubtedly the most decisive event in this respect was the Islamic Revolution in Iran in 1979. Ayatollah Khomeini's ideology powerfully combined modern revolutionary themes, including anti-imperialism and anti-Americanism, with the more traditional language of Islam, thus creating a political 'package' that attracted followers amongst all social and economic classes. Spurred by its success in taking power, the new Iranian regime set out to spread its revolution across the Islamic world. Its primary targets were other countries in which Shiites represented a sizeable portion of the population but, with the exception of Lebanon where the Iranian government was involved in the founding of Hezbollah,[72] it failed to score any quick and/or lasting victories. Similar efforts to 'export' the Iranian model to other (predominantly Sunni) Arab countries were even less successful. Still, one must not underestimate the psychological impact of the Iranian revolution. As Guido Steinberg explains:

> This was the first time that Islamists succeeded in taking over a state. Consider also, this had been a state in which the government – as a result of high oil prices, an effective security service, and a strong alliance with the United States – had seemed invincible. [The Iranian Islamists'] success set an example not just for Shiite but also for Sunni Islamists across the entire Muslim world.[73]

The Iranian revolution, in other words, had proved that political Islam could be powerful and victorious. It provided a blueprint and, more importantly, it changed the discourse among Islamists all over the Muslim world: the question was no longer *whether* political Islam could take power, but *how* this could best be achieved.

The Iranian revolution also launched a religious 'arms race'. Khomeini and his followers saw themselves as champions of the disinherited, and they were as outspokenly critical of the Middle Eastern monarchies and authoritarian regimes, which they viewed as corrupt and un-Islamic, as they were of the West. Middle Eastern regimes, in turn, felt threatened by the popular excitement that had been caused by the Iranian revolution as well as Tehran's efforts to 'export' its brand of political Islam. This perception was particularly acute in Saudi Arabia whose government regarded itself as the ultimate guardian of the faith. After the oil crisis of 1973, the Saudis had spent hundreds of millions of their 'petrodollars' on spreading their own, extremely purist version of Islam, often referred to as Wahhabi. With the Iranian revolution – as well as an uprising of Saudi dissidents in November 1979 – the Saudis' perceived need to shore up their legitimacy became even more urgent. According to Kepel:

> The Iranian revolution's propaganda . . . incited [people] to rise up against the impiety of their leaders, despite their claim to be following the dictates of the Koran and the sharia. The Saudi policy, on the other hand, [was] to finance the expansion of Islamism around the world, the better to control it . . . and to prevent groups bent on changing the status quo from appropriating Islam to themselves.[74]

The Wahhabi brand of Islam may have been less explicitly revolutionary than its Iranian counterpart, but it also called for the implementation of shariah law and encouraged followers to adopt customs that were completely incompatible with life in a modern society.[75] In either case, therefore, the loser in the competition between the Iranian regime and the Saudis was secularism. Indeed, a majority of contemporary Islamist terrorist groups have managed to combine the zeal of the Iranian revolution with the theological purism of the Saudi Wahhabis.

Turning to violence

The year 1979 was a turning point for another reason as well. It was the year in which the Soviet Union invaded Afghanistan which – from the perspective of Islamists across the Muslim world – represented an attack on the *ummah* and, thus, provided a clear justification for (armed) jihad. The event was experienced as highly traumatic, and young, idealistic Islamists everywhere wanted to help the Afghans in expelling the foreign occupiers. (This, of course, included a Saudi named Osama bin Laden who was in his early twenties.) They were mobilized – directly and indirectly – by a coalition consisting of Saudi Arabia, Pakistan and the United States, with the latter keen to 'give the USSR its own Vietnam war'.[76] Precise figures are impossible to obtain, but it is estimated that a total of around 25,000 so-called foreign fighters, mostly from Arab countries, went to Afghanistan over the course of the 1980s.[77] The impact they had on the outcome of the war may have been less significant than they themselves came to believe,[78] but the Afghan experience had a profound impact on the direction of the Islamist movement. Not only did the mujahidin score a triumphant victory, humbling a superpower which – shortly afterwards – went into terminal decline. The anti-Soviet jihad also mobilized, trained and networked an elite corps of Islamist fighters, who had been brutalized in years of conflict and returned to their home countries in high spirits but with no obvious next mission. Indeed, while some decided to be on 'standby' for another invasion of Muslim lands by foreign occupiers, others concluded that it was now time to overthrow the 'apostate', 'ignorant' rulers of their own countries.[79]

The conditions, which existed at the end of the 1980s, made for a perfect storm. The key tenets of political Islam had been disseminated among the populations of the Muslim world for two decades, and popular Islamist opposition movements had sprung up in many countries. The victory in Afghanistan had

buoyed Islamists' confidence, and a fully trained and mobilized network ready to engage in revolutionary violence had
been created. Furthermore, by the time the Cold War ended,
Islamists had convinced themselves that there was a unique
window of opportunity in which to reshape the political land-
scape of the Muslim world. In those countries that were part
of the Eastern bloc, the transition was obvious and tangible.
But even in parts of the Muslim world that used to be associated with the West, Islamists sensed that a new chapter of
history was about to be written and that political Islam had the
opportunity to become an important part of the story. Simply
put, the idea of creating a 'new world order' had excited not
just western policy makers but also the Islamists.[80]

The triggers, which caused the movement's 'violent turn',
are well documented. In Algeria, the Islamist movement
had won a first round of national elections in 1992 but,
anticipating that they would also win the second round, the
government cancelled the whole process and thus denied the
Islamist movement an important opportunity to take power
by democratic means. At about the same time, the Muslim
Brotherhood in Egypt had become by far the largest opposition
movement, yet its ability to participate in national elections
and bring about 'regime change' through legitimate means
was blocked by a government which had largely excluded the
Islamists from the electoral process and often subjected them
to harsh repression under the country's 'emergency laws'.
Moreover, the first Gulf War in 1990–91, during which an
international coalition led by the United States expelled Iraqi
troops from Kuwait and – thereafter – retained a presence in
Saudi Arabia, was regarded as a humiliating insult by many
Islamists who believed that there should be no 'infidel' troops
in the 'Land of the Two Holy Mosques'.

Despite the ominous signs, two of the most recognized
and authoritative scholars in the field, Olivier Roy and Gilles

Kepel, published influential books at the turn of the century which argued that political Islam was in decline (Kepel) and/ or that it had failed (Roy).[81] Though their respective arguments differed, both came to the conclusion that Muslims were getting disillusioned with the idea of political Islam, realizing that it was not possible to run a country according to religious principles.

Neither of them appeared to consider that it tends to be precisely at such points of crisis – that is, when leaders sense that their message is not 'getting through', or that their path to power has been blocked – that radical opposition movements are most likely to consider the use of violence, which may be perceived as a 'game-changer' through which to alter the discourse and revive a revolutionary movement's chances. They were both right, of course, in arguing that the Islamist movement had reached a strategic crossroads but, rather than decline and disappear, parts of the movement responded to the perceived crisis by taking a 'violent turn'. Indeed, in nearly every Arab country, the 1990s saw the formation of Islamist terrorist groups, often led by or drawing on the expertise of the former Afghan Arabs.

The most virulent campaigns of violence were fought in Algeria – leading to a civil war in which more than 100,000 people died – and Egypt, where the government did not rest until it had completely crushed the Islamic Group (Gamaat Islamiya).[82] Furthermore, towards the middle of the decade, radical Islam underwent a process of globalization and transnationalization whereby the emphasis shifted from toppling dictators in the Middle East (the 'near enemy') to fighting those, mainly in the West, who were believed to help them maintain their grip on power (the 'far enemy')[83] (see chapter 3). Radical Islamists, in other words, were active on all fronts: they were confronting 'apostate' rules in the Middle East; they were participating in insurgencies in places like Bosnia,

Chechnya and Kashmir; and they were plotting to attack western targets abroad, beginning with the first attack on the World Trade Center in February 1993.[84] Not all these campaigns were the work of Al Qaeda, but nearly all of them drew on the skills, experience and military leadership of the Afghan Arabs – a resource which some of the states who came under attack had (inadvertently) helped to create. More importantly, though ideological differences between the various groups and their campaigns were considerable, they were all inspired by the same set of ideas which had its roots in the opposition to modernity and globalization and whose popular expression had been suppressed.[85]

The September 11 attacks proved to be the 'game-changer' for which some Islamists had hoped. As Kepel and Roy had correctly noticed, prior to the attacks in 2001, people in the Muslim world were beginning to doubt whether Islamism – which had brought so much violence, death and instability to countries like Egypt and Algeria – was a plausible alternative to the status quo. But the attacks as well as the West's forceful intervention in this 'debate' – in particular its aggressive attempts to hoist western forms of government onto Middle Eastern countries – recreated the fault lines which had given rise to political Islam in the first place. Perhaps policy makers in Washington DC genuinely believed that they were doing people in the Middle East a favour by 'freeing' them from the yoke of dictators such as Saddam Hussein but they clearly understood little about the history of political Islam and the search for cultural authenticity from which it had sprung. Rather than weakening the perception that democracy was a neo-colonialist plot, the western response to the September 11 attack strengthened it, reaffirming the suspicion that the loudly proclaimed War on Terror was, in reality, a war against Islam. It confirmed the Islamists' rhetoric and, in doing so, threw political Islam a lifeline which some of the supposedly 'moderate'

Islamists, especially the Muslim Brotherhood, have skilfully exploited as a way of broadening their movement. The recent excesses of groups like Al Qaeda in Iraq may have prompted majorities in the Muslim world to turn against terrorism as a means of pursuing political change but the political ideology which has underpinned their campaigns is far from dead.

The case of political Islam, like all the other examples mentioned in this chapter, shows that the rise of religiously inspired terrorism did not occur in isolation from broader social and political trends. Nor was it a contradiction of the ideas and developments that were underpinning late modernity and globalization. On the contrary, the religious revival – to which contemporary, religiously inspired terrorism can be traced – constituted a more or less consistent response to the feelings of insecurity and uncertainty that were caused by the forces which late modernity and globalization had unleashed. Religion offered a sense of clarity, direction and purpose in a rapidly changing global environment and – like nationalism – it provided people with a source of identity. Though seemingly anachronistic, the religious revival and the groups and movements it generated must therefore be seen as thoroughly modern in their genesis and manifestations.

In trying to establish what has pushed some of these movements into the political sphere, it is – again – the encounter with modernity and globalization that provided the most obvious 'breeding ground'. The perceived failure of secular ideologies and the widening gap between religious lifestyles and secular reality prompted the religious revivalists to claim back what they believed had been lost. In many cases, this demanded a radical transformation of society according to religious principles, regardless of whether this was desired by a majority of the population or not. Needless to say, only some of these movements ended up taking a 'violent turn'. Their pathways into violence were determined by leaders' strategic choices, the presence of so-called triggers and other mobilizing factors. The example of the American-Christian Army of God illustrated how the process of violent radicalization can play out in practice, and – especially – how different forms of activation and organization have influenced the shape, size and success of the group's campaign.

In many ways, however, the rise of religiously inspired terrorism has complicated the task of understanding the origins of the new terrorism. Religion tends to be associated with peace and moderation, yet the new terrorism hypothesis claims that the return of religiously inspired terrorism has been further complicated by a rise in mass-casualty attacks. How can this make sense? Some of the reasons – for example, the ease with which religion allows distinctions between the in-group and the 'other' – have been hinted at. However, as will be argued in the following chapter, focusing on religion alone will not be sufficient in explaining more fundamental developments which, again, have their roots in late modernity and globalization.

CHAPTER FIVE

Dying to Kill? The Rise of Mass-Casualty Terrorism

Since the September 11 attacks in 2001, much attention has focused on the phenomenon of the suicide bomber. Numerous books have been written about the psychology of individuals who are willing to put themselves forward for missions in which they are certain to die.[1] What are the 'root causes' of suicide terrorism?[2] Why are people 'dying to kill'?[3] In reality, there is nothing remarkable at all in the idea of dying for a cause – except perhaps that late modern, western minds find it hard to accept that anyone would believe in anything strongly enough to make the ultimate sacrifice. History is littered with examples of men (and women) who were willing to put their lives on the line in order to make a difference to the cause they believed in.[4] This is true not only for the Kamikaze pilots of the Second World War but also for millions of ordinary soldiers who were deployed on missions they knew they had virtually no chance of surviving.[5]

Even for terrorists, the idea of dying for a cause is nothing particularly novel or noteworthy and long precedes the advent of the suicide bomber. All Irish Republican Army (IRA) volunteers, for example, were warned that membership of the organization was most likely to result in capture or death.[6] In 1981, ten Irish Republicans starved themselves to death in order to achieve political status for their fellow prisoners and were immediately regarded as 'martyrs' by their followers and sympathizers. Indeed, terrorist groups and non-violent resistance organizations all over the world have used hunger strikes as a means of forcing concessions or drawing attention to their cause.

What distinguishes the hunger striker from the suicide bomber is not the willingness or expectation to die for a cause – arguably, both tactics represent a form of voluntary death[7]– but the number of people killed in the process. Whereas the hunger striker only kills himself (or herself), the aim of the suicide bomber is to kill others. In fact, many suicide bombers have been deployed precisely in order to facilitate access to targets that allow for the killing of people who – by any reasonable standard – would be described as innocent civilians. In other words, it is the shift in targets, not the identity or the motivation of the perpetrator, that constitutes the novelty.

This chapter looks at the reasons behind the increase in lethality and brutality which has marked the new terrorism. In the first section, it will be shown how late modernity and globalization have led to a decline of universalist ideas and ideologies, which in turn has facilitated the targeting of populations representing the 'other' by nationalist, racist and religiously motivated groups. The second section draws on developments in information technology and the media, showing how it has become increasingly difficult to grab an audience's attention and how the new media environment offers incentives for terrorist groups to engage in ever more spectacular and brutal attacks.

The decline of universalism

In trying to make sense of the rise of mass-casualty terrorism, it is necessary to take another look at how terrorist aims and ideologies have evolved.[8] As shown in chapter 2, the rise of religiously inspired ideologies is one of the defining features of the new terrorism. But religiously motivated terrorism is not the dominant or exclusive ideological manifestation of terrorism today, and its novelty does not mean that all other forms of terrorism have been sidelined or marginalized. The analyst Ekaterina Stepanova points out that there is no firm evidence that religion has overtaken nationalism or separatism as the most 'popular' cause in whose name acts of terrorism are carried out. Especially at the domestic level, 'radical nationalism remains as powerful a mobilization tool for armed non-state actors as religious extremism'.[9]

The continued strength of nationalism should come as no surprise. The break-up of federations such as Yugoslavia and the Soviet Union after the end of the Cold War has created new minorities and, with them, new grievances that have been translated into some of the most vociferous ethnic conflicts since the Second World War. Meanwhile, many of the 'older' nationalist conflicts, such as in Sri Lanka or the Basque Country, remain unresolved. It is, of course, difficult to say exactly by how much nationalist terrorism has increased or decreased: many databases do not count 'domestic' terrorist incidents, and reliable statistics are nearly impossible to obtain from many of the places in which the most virulent confrontations have taken place (for example, Chechnya). Still, if one looks at the most recent report of the US National Counterterrorism Center, it becomes obvious that nationalist/separatist terrorism, whether in India, the Philippines, Sri Lanka or other places, is still very much alive.[10]

In turn, the one type of ideological inspiration for terrorism which has notably declined is Marxism. For most westerners and Latin Americans in the 1970s and 1980s, terrorism used to be synonymous with the activities of Marxist-inspired groups like the Red Army Faction in Germany, the Red Brigades in Italy, Action Directe in France, the Weathermen in the United States or the Tupamaros in Uruguay. None of these groups any longer exist. In fact, the only significant left-wing groups which have survived the end of the Soviet Union and continue to engage in violence can be found in Colombia.[11] In many other places, the mixture of Marxism and nationalism, which typified so many struggles for national liberation in the 1970s and 1980s, has been replaced by a combination of religion and nationalism. As mentioned in chapter 2, the conflicts in Kashmir or the Palestinian Territories are still being fought in the name of national liberation, but the terrorists' idea of national liberation no longer includes any element of class struggle.

Why does this matter? Comparing the kinds of ideological drivers that have retained their position (nationalism) or increased in importance (religion) with those that have declined (left-wing ideologies), it becomes obvious that there has been a shift from 'universalist' to 'particularist' ideologies. Nationalist and religiously inspired ideologies are particularist because they divide people according to whether they share the same ethnicity, belief or birthplace: 'believers' or 'compatriots' whose customs, attitudes or even appearances are closer to one's own are regarded as superior, whereas 'foreigners' or 'unbelievers' are not only viewed as inferior but seen as a threat to one's own identity.[12] Left-wing ideologies, on the other hand, are universalist because they are committed to humanistic ideals, such as equality and human dignity, and driven by the vision of a world in which national, ethnic, religious and racial divisions no longer play any role. Needless to say, these ideals have frequently been at odds with the actions of left-wing terrorists who have been responsible for killing large numbers of people and Marxist governments which have engaged in large-scale repression and, sometimes, indiscriminate violence. Still, as will be shown, the stated commitment to universalist ideals has often made it more difficult for terrorists with a left-wing orientation to engage in seemingly random violence against civilians based merely on their ethnic, religious or national affiliations.

During the era of old terrorism, the only terrorists who clearly and unambiguously followed the particularist paradigm were right-wing terrorists who had no hesitation in killing large numbers of civilians when they belonged to the ethnic or racial 'other'. The 'red' terrorists, such as the Red Brigades or Action Directe, while carrying out numerous kidnappings and targeted assassinations, largely adhered to the (Russian anarchist) maxim that 'not one drop of superfluous blood' should be spilled.[13] Likewise, for most of the 'old' nationalists, who mixed (particularist) nationalism with (universalist) Marxism, there existed constraints which helped to keep their particularist instincts in check. By contrast, in the era of new terrorism, such constraints are no longer significant. As mentioned above, even where terrorist groups have multiple agendas, these agendas are now more likely to consist of different varieties of particularism – nationalism and religion – than combine particularist with universalist ideas, with the result that members of the out-group are no longer also considered 'workers' or 'comrades' but exclusively seen as 'others' who pose a threat and against whom any action may be justified.

To illustrate the argument, it will be useful to introduce a number of case studies. The following sections will apply: the 'particularism vs. universalism' prism to recent debates within Al Qaeda; the alleged involvement of Basque Homeland and Liberty (ETA) in the Madrid bombings in 2004; and the differences in targeting policy between Republicans and Loyalists in Northern Ireland.

Republicans and Loyalists in Northern Ireland
A particularly interesting and relevant example are the Loyalist and Irish Republican terrorist groups in Northern Ireland. Loyalist and Republican groups are often portrayed as two sides of the same coin because they fought on behalf of the two ethnic

communities that were in conflict. The Loyalists – represented, most prominently, by the Ulster Volunteer Force (UVF) and the Ulster Defence Association (UDA) – were Ulster and/or British nationalists who wanted to keep Northern Ireland as part of the United Kingdom, whereas the Republicans – represented primarily by the IRA – were Irish nationalists, who wanted the province to join with the Irish Republic. In ideological terms, however, there was a clear difference. As shown in chapter 2, Irish Republicans combined nationalist with left-wing ideologies, drawing on republican influences that reached back to the time of the French Revolution as well as a tradition of left-wing and trade union activism that originated in the late nineteenth and early twentieth centuries. Loyalists, on the other hand, had no distinct ideological agenda at all other than the desire to preserve their British cultural identity and for Northern Ireland to remain part of the United Kingdom. Theirs was a particularist ideology, which defined the (Protestant) British population of the province as part of the in-group and the Catholics as the 'other' whose claims and nationalist aspirations had to be resisted. Loyalists were mostly not inspired by religion,[14] nor are they generally regarded as representatives of the 'new' terrorism. In fact, it is precisely because there is nothing 'new' about the Loyalists' campaigns other than their particularist agenda that makes their case so valuable.

The IRA and its campaign were described in detail in chapter 2. It is worth reiterating that, despite some instances of brutality and the very considerable death toll that was caused by its activities, the IRA was not a terrorist group which routinely engaged in mass-casualty attacks. On the contrary, there were only seven incidents in its thirty-year campaign in which the group killed ten or more people. Of these, two were mistakes whilst a further three were directed at military targets that were seen as legitimate acts of war by the IRA and its constituency. Only two of the seven attacks could be construed as 'sectarian'; that is, they involved the killing of innocent civilians for no reason other than their ethnic affiliation. No doubt, there were several periods during the conflict – in the mid-1970s or the early 1990s, for example – when it appeared as if the campaign was adopting a more particularist character. Taken as a whole, though, the campaign never tipped over into outright sectarianism.

The contrast with the Loyalist campaign could not be starker. Some of the Loyalist campaigns grew out of vigilante committees that had been formed to protect Protestant neighbourhoods against IRA attacks. Very soon, however, the Loyalists started to engage in systematic 'tit for tat' killings whereby innocent Catholics would be killed in retaliation for IRA attacks. Typically, the Loyalists would pick up random individuals in Catholic areas, drive them to a quiet spot and execute them. Loyalist groups also carried out large-scale bomb attacks, often against civilian targets. The UVF's bombings in the Republic of Ireland in May 1974, for example, targeted the Dublin shopping district during the afternoon rush hour as well as a pub in County Monaghan, killing a pensioner, a teenage girl and a baby among others.[15] Following such attacks, Loyalist leaders would try to rationalize their foot soldiers' activities as a form of deterrence or blame them on a lack of discipline.[16] In reality, though, the driving factor seems to have been the burning desire to exact a form of revenge against Catholics who – as a community – were regarded as complicit with the IRA. The following excerpt from a conversation between the BBC's Peter Taylor and a former member of the UDA illustrates the Loyalists' attitude:

> *UDA member*: I was angry and wanted to do just as much damage to the community responsible for those actions . . . Doing twice the amount of damage that they were doing in my community.

> *Peter Taylor:* But it wasn't the Catholic community that planted the bombs, it was the IRA that did it.
>
> *UDA member:* I think you're right about that, but that's not how I saw it then. I would have linked it into other events that were taking place and would have seen it as . . . being done on their behalf. So they were part of it.[17]

It should be pointed out, of course, that Republicans killed nearly three times as many people as Loyalists, and instances of 'othering' and sectarianism could also be found among IRA members. Nevertheless, it is equally true that, in marked contrast to the IRA, the Loyalist campaigns consisted of very little else but sectarian attacks.

As explained in chapter 2, there always existed a tension between the IRA's own analysis of the conflict, which identified British imperialism as the main culprit, and the views of its sympathizers, who regarded the IRA mainly as a Catholic defence force. Indeed, it was the latter, more particularist, role from which the IRA derived much of its support and legitimacy within the Catholic community. Also, there can be no question that many of the young men who decided to join the IRA were driven by motives that were quite similar to the sentiments expressed by the UDA member cited above, namely a hatred of the 'other' community and the desire to 'pay back'. At the same time, it seems clear that, upon entering the organization, the leadership made genuine efforts to 're-educate' their recruits about the 'true' nature of the conflict, diverting their attention from the Protestant community to what it believed were the 'underlying forces' that had brought about the conflict.

The IRA's training manual – the so-called Green Book – taught recruits that the enemy that needed to be fought was the British government and the ruling classes that benefited from the structures of political and economic exploitation which the 'imperial arrangement' had created. Accordingly, 'enemies of the people' that stood in the way of creating a 'Democratic Socialist Republic' included not only the British government and the 'ruling classes' in Northern Ireland but also, for example, the Catholic middle class in whose economic interest it was to maintain the constitutional status quo.[18] In fact, Republican publications often stressed that the 'Protestant working class are our brothers and sisters' with whom Catholic workers needed to join in order to create a new Ireland.[19] This attitude may have been shallow, patronizing and ignorant of the Protestants' strong sense of British identity,[20] but it added a universalist dimension which appears to have prevented the IRA from slipping into an overtly sectarian campaign.

By contrast, Loyalist political attitudes were less developed than the Republicans'. Loyalists, after all, were defending the status quo, which meant that – from their point of view – it was not necessary to develop and embrace a new political project.[21] More importantly, most of the Loyalist campaigns had arisen out of the need to defend Protestant areas against IRA incursions. Faced with the 'other', the narrative of communal conflict provided all the justification and rationalization that was required. As the academics Joseph Ruane and Jennifer Todd explain:

> Contemporary events were seen in terms of images of the past: Protestants were being pushed out of their traditional areas and workplaces [by Catholics], they were under siege, subject to genocidal attack, forced to retaliate. Only loyalist organisation, vigilance and militancy could defend the Protestant population.[22]

For Loyalists, this was a time for action rather than grand ideological debates. Loyalists were conscious of their working-class status, and they frequently articulated their dismay about having been used as 'cannon fodder' by the Unionist establishment in the past. No Loyalist leader, however, ever expressed such sentiments in a coherent fashion, and – until the peace process of the 1990s – they never translated into any sense of cross-sectarian solidarity.[23] As a result, there was hardly anything in Loyalist ideology that would have moderated the terrorists' particularist orientation. Unlike the IRA, young Protestants who joined the UDA or the UVF were given free rein to pursue their sectarian instincts.

ETA and the Madrid bombings

A more recent example is the case of ETA and its alleged involvement in the Madrid train attacks of 2004 which killed 191 people. In its fifty-year campaign for an independent Basque homeland to contain several provinces in today's Spain and France, ETA has killed more than 800 people.[24] ETA is mostly known as a Basque separatist organization but, like the IRA, it has always called for both national independence and socialism.

Throughout ETA's history, the tension between nationalist/particularist and left-wing/universalist tendencies has caused numerous conflicts and resulted in a series of splits.[25] At its fourth Assembly in 1965, for example, ETA decided in favour of a distinctly Marxist outlook, arguing that the Basque Country could only ever be truly free if its workers had been liberated. A year later, this approach was reversed and a more traditional, nationalist agenda was adopted. In the summer of 1970, a new leadership yet again chose to make the working-class issue a priority. It virtually abandoned the nationalist agenda and, instead, decided to create a revolutionary worker's party that would mobilize the masses and trigger a revolution across the Iberian peninsula. ETA started kidnapping prominent businessmen whose release was made conditional upon the payment of the ransom as well as the successful resolution of industrial disputes. According to the journalist Paddy Woodworth, 'while ETA filled its war chest, it enjoyed the considerable prestige of playing Robin Hood to striking workers'.[26]

During Spain's transition from authoritarian rule to democracy in the mid-1970s, many of the Marxists left the organization and decided to pursue their political aims through the democratic process. Yet even the nationalist ETA core, which continued the terrorist campaign in the 1980s and 1990s, consisted mainly of committed socialists who were, by and large, sincere about their desire to see a social as well as a national revolution.[27] In fact, when ETA's political wing, Batasuna, was declared illegal by the Spanish government in 2003, the leadership entered into an agreement with the Communist Party of the Basque Lands which agreed to follow ETA's political platform in return for the group's endorsement at the Basque regional elections. In other words, even when most of the doctrinaire Marxists had left the group, the commitment to left-wing ideals continued to be upheld.

In the course of its terrorist campaign, ETA has carried out only a small number of attacks in which large numbers of civilians were killed. In terms of fatalities, the worst attack was the bombing of a supermarket car park in Barcelona in June 1987 which killed 21 people, including several small children. Only one other attack – the bombing of a cafeteria in Madrid in September 1974 – cost the lives of more than ten civilians.[28] ETA usually provides warnings, and most of the (random) civilian casualties were the result of inadequate warnings or careless planning. For example, when ETA blew up a residential compound of the Spanish military police in May 1991, it failed to take into account that the building was located next to a school. As a consequence, of the ten people that were killed, four were children that had been attending classes at the time of the explosion. Needless to say, the frequency with which such 'mistakes' occurred demonstrates a high degree of ruthlessness on behalf of ETA but it still needs to be recognized that the group was not, as a matter of principle, aiming to kill random Spaniards merely because they belonged to the 'other' ethnic group. Unlike the Loyalists in Northern Ireland, for instance, ETA clearly had no intention of making the Spanish population *as a whole* pay for what they saw as the oppression of the Basque people and the continued occupation of Basque lands by the Spanish government. Considering ETA's capabilities as a terrorist organization, if this had been the intention, one would have expected to see a far higher number of attacks against 'soft' targets over the course of nearly fifty years in which ETA has been in existence.

Again, as in the case of the IRA, it is important to emphasize that, despite refraining from mass-casualty attacks against civilians, ETA has not been running its campaign according to Queensberry rules. Nor has the organization necessarily been committed to pluralism or democratic principles. On the contrary, a significant proportion of the civilians that have been killed in ETA attacks were officials or politicians that had been elected by the very people on whose behalf ETA claimed to fight or, quite simply, individuals who happened to disagree with the organization and its aims. In 1997, for example, millions of Spaniards joined demonstrations against ETA when the group abducted and killed a local councillor from the Basque country, Miguel Angel Blanco, whose only crime appears to have been his opposition to ETA. Even in recent years, the group has targeted Basque academics and journalists who have spoken out against ETA and were consequently considered 'enemies of the Basque people'. Such actions betray the group's intolerant and paranoid mindset which years of involvement in 'armed struggle' have only made worse. It would be wrong, therefore, to look at groups such as ETA – or indeed the IRA – as 'knights in shining armour' merely because there now exist other groups whose campaigns are even less discriminating.

Against this background, it might not have been completely impossible – but it certainly must have seemed very unlikely – for ETA to be responsible for the terrorist attacks in Madrid in March 2004. The Madrid train attacks consisted of ten rucksack bombs that had been left on four commuter trains during the morning rush hour. There were no warnings. The Spanish government initially accused ETA, saying that the type of explosives used and a recently thwarted attack against a train station in Madrid made ETA the most likely perpetrators. But it soon turned out that the real culprit was a group of Islamist extremists, who might have taken their cue from Al Qaeda (see chapter 3). Regarding the attackers' motivation and ideology, the most telling statement came twenty-four hours after the attack when the so-called Abu Hafs Al Masri Brigades – a *nom de guerre* frequently used in connection with Al Qaeda-inspired attacks – issued a letter, which declared: 'We . . . have not felt sad for the so-called civilians. Is it OK for you to kill our children, women, old people and youth in Afghanistan, Iraq, Palestine and Kashmir? And is it forbidden to us to kill yours?'[29] It is unclear whether the letter's authors had any direct connection with the attackers, but its content clearly illustrated the particularist mindset that underlies Al Qaeda's terrorist campaign. It suggested that just about everyone who happens to live in a 'Crusader' nation is a legitimate target for 'retaliation' against enemy governments. In fact, it seems as if, for the particularists associated with Al Qaeda, even the many immigrant workers from countries like Peru, Cuba and Ecuador who were making their way to central Madrid that morning had forfeited the right to be considered 'innocent'.

The numbers alone should have made it obvious that ETA was not likely to be involved. As Woodworth explained, 'The bombs in Madrid claimed twice as many victims in one morning as ETA had ever claimed in an entire year and nine times as many as the group had killed in any single atrocity.'[30] As a result, even some of ETA's fiercest critics felt compelled to defend the group. Two days after the bombings, when the Spanish government still stood by its claim that ETA was responsible, the leader of a Basque peace group pointed out, 'These attacks just did not fit with the strategy and logic of ETA . . . It has never deliberately sought to kill civilians, and it always sends a warning'.[31] It was true that ETA had planned a number of attacks on public transport facilities but, had the plans succeeded, the operations would have been carried out in a completely different manner. Given ETA's record, there is a good chance that some civilians might have been killed or wounded as a result of bad planning, but it is nearly inconceivable that the number of fatalities would have reached triple digits. The explanation for this restraint was provided by ETA itself. In statements released immediately after the attacks, the group said it would 'never' attack Spanish workers whom it considered to be allies in the struggle against imperialism. Indeed, one of the leaders of Batasuna told newspapers that 'there's a big difference' between ETA's modus operandi and the idea of 'attacking trains carrying people into work from working-class areas'.[32] However misguided and ruthless, ETA's commitment to universalist values had made it impossible for the group to 'other' civilians based merely on their ethnic or national identification.

Debates within Al Qaeda

The case of Al Qaeda requires further exploration. In the previous chapter, it was established that, just because its ideology is inspired by religion, Al Qaeda does not exist in a political vacuum. Indeed, as will be shown, Münkler's suggestion that the new terrorism is different from the old because it is no longer responsive to – and restrained by – any real-world constituency ignores much of the debate that has been taking place within Al Qaeda over the past years.[33] Al Qaeda's constituency may not be geographically bound in the same way in which most of the supporters of ETA and the IRA can all be found in the same place. (In fact, Al Qaeda's 'base' may no longer be located in any physically defined territory but, rather, in virtual space.) But there clearly exists a wider constituency to whom the group is accountable and whose views the leadership aims to anticipate.

The September 11 attacks against the United States are a good example. From a western perspective, bringing down the Twin Towers may have seemed like a truly 'mindless' act of violence which no reasonable person could approve of but, in large parts of the Muslim world, the attacks were quite popular and helped turn bin Laden into the most powerful symbol of defiance against the West and America in particular. In a secretly taped conversation, which was released several weeks following the attacks, bin Laden could be seen telling his associates how delighted he was that the attack had sparked renewed interest in Islam in countries as far away as the United States and Holland. He also enquired about 'the stand of the mosques' in Saudi Arabia, and made it clear that the attacks were meant to be a symbolic statement. In his own words, 'Those young men [inaudible] said in deeds, in New York and Washington, speeches that overshadowed all other speeches made everywhere else in the world. The speeches are understood by both Arabs and non-Arabs – even by Chinese.'[34] These comments not only demonstrated that bin Laden was intrigued by how his actions had been received in the Muslim world but also, and more importantly, that he conceived of his organization as a form of vanguard whose spectacular acts of violence were designed to incite and inspire others to follow its lead.

Having a constituency, however, does not necessarily make Al Qaeda universalists. It is often said that Al Qaeda has been confronted with a huge backlash from within its own constituency because of the large numbers of innocents it has killed. If one examines these debates more closely, however, it becomes obvious that it is not civilians per se but, rather, *Muslims* which many Al Qaeda's sympathizers are concerned about.

Realizing that the group had been losing some of its support, Al Qaeda's deputy leader, Ayman al Zawahiri, agreed to participate in a virtual question-and-answer session in late 2007 during which he responded to the concerns of Al Qaeda sympathizers from across the world. One of the world's leading Al Qaeda experts, Lawrence Wright, looked at the exchange in detail and concluded that most of the unhappiness among Al Qaeda's grassroots was caused not by its violent actions against Christians or Jews but by the numbers of Muslims it was killing.[35] The first questioner demanded to know: 'Who is it who is killing . . . the innocents in Baghdad, Morocco and Algeria? . . . Why have you not – to this day – carried out any strike in Israel? Or is it easier to kill Muslims in the markets?' Another questioner wanted Al Zawahiri to explain what had justified the killing of 60 Algerian army recruits by Al Qaeda's affiliate, Al Qaeda in the Islamic Maghreb. Al Zawahiri responded, quite plausibly, by saying that – though technically Muslims – the victims of the attack had been defending 'the Crusader unbelievers' and should therefore be considered apostates and traitors.[36]

Nevertheless, there have been signs that the group's particularist paradigm is being challenged. Following the London transport attacks in July 2005, for instance, Al Qaeda sympathizers engaged in a stormy online debate about the justification for the bombings. The discussion was initiated by a leading Islamist thinker, Abu Basir, who had condoned Al Qaeda-inspired attacks in the past but decided to condemn the attacks in London unreservedly. He argued that the bombings were 'shameful' and 'devoid of any manliness, courage and moral'.[37] In his view, British civilians could not be defined as legitimate targets based merely on the policies of their government. Unwittingly echoing the debates between particularists and universalists from Northern Ireland to the Basque Country, Basir stated that Islamic law did not know the concept of 'collective revenge', and that – to the contrary – the Koran demanded the protection of civilians.[38] Those who supported the London attacks, on the other hand, cited the arguments that had also been used to justify the attacks in New York and Madrid. Indeed, one of the participants claimed that it was not permissible for Muslims to feel any kind of pity for unbelievers.[39] It may be difficult to say who 'won' the argument, but it is worth noting that, even among committed Al Qaeda sympathizers, who clearly had been prepared to defend even the most atrocious attacks against civilians a few years back, doubts about the idea of engaging in 'collective revenge' against the religious 'other' appears to have crept in.

On an even larger scale, this emerging debate between particularists and universalists could be seen in the context of the so-called Revisions that were published by the former leader of the Egyptian terrorist group Al Jihad, Sayyid Imam Al Sharif a.k.a. 'Dr Fadl'. Parts of Fadl's condemnation of Al Qaeda's attacks rests on the particularist premise that, even when targeting foreigners who were likely to be 'unbelievers', one can never be absolutely sure because some of them may be Muslim. According to Fadl, 'You cannot decide who is a Muslim or who is an unbeliever or who should be killed based on the colour of his skin or hair or the language he speaks . . . There are no proper indications for who is a Muslim and who is not.'[40] More significantly, he then constructs an Islamist version of universalism, which may not go as far as recognizing the equality and human rights of every person but at least concedes that

> there is nothing in the Sharia about killing Jews and the
> Nazarenes [Christians], referred to by some as the Crusaders
> . . . they are the neighbors [sic] of Muslims . . . and being
> kind to one's neighbors is a Muslim duty . . . There is no
> legal reason for harming people in any way. [Indeed, if] vice
> is mixed with virtue, all becomes sinful.[41]

Considering Fadl's credentials as one of the forefathers of the
Al Qaeda movement, the kind of argument presented in the
'Revisions' was a small revolution. In Wright's words, Fadl
did nothing less than '[undermine] the entire intellectual
framework of jihadist warfare'.[42] Unsurprisingly, Fadl's intervention sparked an intensive debate and prompted Zawahiri
to issue a series of scathing criticisms. For Zawahiri, it must
have been obvious that, if Fadl managed to convince Al
Qaeda's constituency of the validity of his case, this would be
the end of Al Qaeda as a popular ideology.

Although there are other important aspects of Al Qaeda's
recent ideological evolution, the debate is best described as
a confrontation between particularist and universalist concepts. It seems clear that, at this point, the majority of Al
Qaeda's supporters still cling to a particularist perspective
and that their criticisms of the Al Qaeda leadership relate not
to the killing of civilians as such but, rather, to the killing of
Muslims. From a counter-terrorist perspective, this kind of
critique may, over time, help to undermine Al Qaeda's leaders
and compel them to try to change the group's modus operandi, but it will not counter the idea on which Al Qaeda rests.

If, however, the universalist argument – advocated by Fadl
and an increasingly significant minority of other opinion
formers within the movement – was to take hold, Al Qaeda
as a project would be in serious jeopardy. Recent US intelligence reports have pointed out that, despite the continued
threat of attacks, Al Qaeda has suffered 'strategic defeats'
in several countries, including Indonesia and a number of

Middle Eastern states.[43] The underlying reason for such optimistic assessments is a growing sense that, among hard-core Islamists in a number of Muslim societies, the balance has been shifting away from the particularist viewpoint. And indeed, if Al Qaeda loses the argument with its constituency, it will have nowhere to go.

One may conclude, therefore, that the decline of universalist ideas over the course of recent decades has played an important role in facilitating mass-casualty attacks against innocent civilians. There can be no doubt that the rise of 'identity ideologies' – centred predominantly around nationalism and religion – has made it easier for terrorists to 'other' enemy populations and has, thus, facilitated their targeting in violent attacks.

At the same time, there have been other significant developments related to late modernity and globalization that cannot be ignored in any attempt to explain the trend towards greater lethality. In fact, as will be shown in the next section, changes in the media environment have also contributed to the rise in mass-casualty attacks.

'Getting through' in the (new) media age

In the aftermath of September 11, many commentators found it impossible to see how the attacks had any communicative purpose at all. In his *New York Times* column, Thomas Friedman speculated that terrorists like bin Laden were no longer using violence 'to grab headlines but [simply] to kill as many Americans as possible'.[44] This statement, like many others, failed to recognize not only that the September 11 attacks had produced some of the most (shockingly) powerful visuals in television history but also that, as noted in chapter 2, terrorism is a form of (vicious) communication. By definition, terrorism relies on the media to amplify the effects of (mostly) limited acts of violence so it can inspire fear and terror in a target audience and inspire followers to take up arms. While this remains true in principle, this section will show that the media age has made it increasingly difficult for the terrorists' message to 'get through'. The new media environment, together with some of the developments described above, has pushed terrorist organizations towards ever more spectacular acts of violence, which – in turn – helps to explain the increase in lethality and brutality that have marked the new terrorism.

Media overload and 'emotional desensitization'

Throughout history, terrorists have responded to developments in the media by adapting their tactics and targets. It may be no accident, for instance, that the concept of the 'propaganda of the deed', which underpinned the campaigns of the Russian anarchists, emerged at a time when mass-circulation newspapers had just become commonplace. Likewise, the rise of television in the late 1950s and 1960s prompted a whole range of new tactics, including, most prominently, the hijackings of aircraft which are often said to have been staged for television audiences. One of the most frequently cited examples is the hijacking of TWA flight 847 in Beirut in 1985. As Brigitte Nacos shows, during the carefully choreographed takeover the reporters who were covering the story were surprised to find that the hijackers knew all about 'the geographic reach of the American media, the audience size of different media types, the working of press pools, and the advantages of scheduling live interviews during TV networks' popular morning and early evening news broadcasts'.[45] By the 1980s, the relationship between terrorists and the media had become virtually 'symbiotic', with terrorists eager to provide the 'mystery, quick action, tension [and] drama' for which the big television networks were longing.[46]

Some of these dynamics continue to shape terrorists' attitudes. But the environment in which they are being played out has changed profoundly. The most obvious difference to earlier periods is that there are far more channels through which people receive (and engage in) communication, which means that there exist more opportunities for terrorists to convey their message, but also that it has become much harder for them to capture an audience's attention. The spread of satellite and digital technology since the late 1980s has prompted the creation of hundreds of new television channels (see chapter 3) and produced entirely new types of media. In 2008, a typical American family was equipped with 'three TV sets, three video players, three radios, three hand-held music devices, two video game consoles, and a personal computer'.[47] In the United States, as in all other industrialized countries, television remains by far the most popular medium but younger audiences especially have come to receive much of their information through other media, in particular the Internet. In fact, according to the latest annual survey by the British communications agency Ofcom, the Internet has, for the first time, overtaken television as the 'most indispensable' medium in the eyes of 16–24 year olds.[48]

To make matters even more complicated, not only has media consumption become more diversified, people are less likely to be shocked or terrified by displays of violence. Various surveys in different countries have shown that the amount of violence on television screens has risen substantially. A Canadian study, for example, found that displays of physical violence on the country's six major television networks had increased by 378 per cent over a seven-year period starting in 1993.[49] Another study, carried out by the British Broadcasting Standards Commission, produced similar results, showing that there had been 'a sharp increase in the amount of violence screened' in the 1998–2001 period.[50]

Many commentators attribute this development to increased competition among new television channels and other media providers who seem to want to shock their audiences into tuning in. This is especially true for television news which is more likely now than in the past to contain gruesome stories and depictions of violent crime. Faced with a demanding 24-hour news cycle, broadcasters appear to have adopted the motto: 'If it bleeds, it leads.'[51]

Needless to say, the debate about violence in the media and its impact on people – especially children – is highly controversial for reasons completely unrelated to terrorism. Yet the accumulated wisdom of nearly five decades of psychological research provides some valuable insight that is relevant to the topic of this book. Most importantly, there exists a consensus among experts that people's increased exposure to violence on television has led to a degree of 'emotional desensitization' that 'occurs when people who watch a lot of media violence no longer respond with as much unpleasant physiological arousal as they did initially'.[52] According to a team of researchers that sifted through hundreds of papers on the issue, this effect has been substantiated in at least half a dozen different studies over the course of several decades.[53] In other words, increasing amounts of violence on television screens have raised the threshold for what is considered 'shocking' or 'terrifying' by the viewing public. For terrorists, the implication is clear. In the words of the French anarchist Auguste Vaillant, who had bombed the French National Assembly in 1893: 'The more they are deaf, the more your voice must thunder out so that they will understand you.'[54]

One of the best contemporary examples for this effect and its consequences for terrorist behaviour are the Oklahoma Bombings of 1995. Following the attacks, Timothy McVeigh was widely portrayed as a right-wing lunatic who had suffered from mental problems following his service in the US

Army during the first Gulf War. In many ways, though, he was a highly intelligent person who invested a great deal of thinking into planning the attacks on the Alfred P. Murrah federal building, that killed 168 people, including 19 children who were attending a daycare centre. Interviewed during his incarceration, McVeigh freely admitted that he had picked the building in Oklahoma because it had 'plenty of open space around it, to allow for the best possible news photos and television footage'.[55] The objective of the bombing, he said, was to send a message, and all his preparations consequently served the purpose of making sure that this message 'was heard around the world'.[56] Unwittingly echoing the words of the French anarchist Vaillant, he said he wanted to 'make the loudest statement . . . and create a stark, horrifying image that would make everyone who saw it stop and take notice'.[57] Indeed, he conceded that, in doing so, it was necessary to kill large numbers of people. Talking to one of the members of his defence team in July 1995, he was confronted with the comments of a fellow anti-government activist who had suggested that, had the bombing taken place at night rather than during the day (thus killing fewer people), the movement would now consider McVeigh a hero. The defence team member reported his reaction as follows: 'Mr McVeigh looked directly into my eyes and told me: "That would not have gotten [sic] the point across . . . We needed a body count to make our point."'[58]

Greater brutality and lethality is by far the most common way for terrorists to 'get the message through' in the media age. It is worth pointing out, however, that some groups have developed other – arguably, more sophisticated – ways in which to shock an increasingly scattered and desensitized audience. For instance, when Palestinian terror groups realized that their target audience had become desensitized to the steady trickle of suicide bombings during the so-called Second Intifada, they started deploying 'unusual' suicide bombers.

Nacos cites the example of Abdul Misk, an imam and devoted father of two whose wife was pregnant with a third child. Following his suicide mission in August 2003, which killed 20 Jewish worshippers in Jerusalem, the *New York Times* printed a long story about Misk together with a picture of him and his children which had been taken only three days before he blew himself up. According to Nacos, 'Here was a compelling image that made people wonder what conditions could drive such a man to become a human bomb. This was precisely the effect that terrorists hope for.'[59] Indeed, Clara Beyler, who analysed public reactions to suicide bombings, believes that the same rationale underlies the deployment of 'female kamikazes'. Women, she argues, tend to be portrayed by the media as 'the symbols of utter despair . . . rather than the cold-blooded murderers of civilians'.[60]

Outbidding

Another factor that has contributed to higher levels of brutality and lethality is what some academics have described as 'outbidding'.[61] Where different terrorist groups or factions compete with each other for a constituency's support, escalating the level of violence may be a promising strategy for gaining an advantage over one's rivals. This obviously works best when one's constituency already supports the use of violence and engaging in acts of terrorism is seen as a positive means of demonstrating commitment. The result of outbidding will be a spiral of violence in which different groups feel compelled to engage in ever more spectacular acts of violence in order to 'top' their rivals' latest attacks. Organizations which had previously refrained from deliberate attacks against civilians may be drawn into mass-casualty attacks simply in order to prove that they are capable of inflicting as much damage as their rivals. Indeed, in such a scenario, ideology may have less

influence over targeting decisions as groups perceive themselves to be in a struggle for survival. Furthermore, once the
'bidding war' is over, it will become more difficult to reduce
the violence to a more 'acceptable' level. The population will
have become desensitized, and the expectation of what constitutes 'terror' in the eyes of the target audience will have shifted
to a higher level. The result is an increased overall threshold of
terror which any subsequent terrorist attacks will need to overcome in order to achieve the desired communicative effects.

Competition and outbidding are not new, of course, but they
are more likely to produce higher levels of lethality and brutality in the era of new terrorism. As mentioned above, people are
more desensitized to violence which means that bidding wars
will escalate from higher levels to begin with. Furthermore,
the competing factions are more likely to include groups with
particularist rather than universalist agendas. In fact, where
universalists are in competition with particularists, outbidding can result in the universalists adopting the methods and
tactics that are favoured by the particularists.

The best-researched case in which this dynamic has unfolded
is the Arab–Israeli conflict. Yasser Arafat's non-religious Fatah
had never engaged in the suicide bombing of civilian targets
but, as the researcher Mia Bloom and others have shown, the
group felt it necessary to employ such tactics when Hamas was
beginning to threaten its hegemony. Hamas had been almost
completely marginalized by Fatah prior to the outbreak of the
Second Intifada in September 2000, and it was only through
the use of large-scale attacks against civilian targets that Hamas
could undermine Fatah's legitimacy and gain so much popular
support that it was perceived as a threat to Yasser Arafat's leadership.[62] Cornered by Hamas, the Fatah leadership responded
by establishing the Al Aqsa Martyrs' Brigades and engaging in
the kind of operations which they had earlier condemned. As
the Israeli scholar Amir Pedahzur explains:

> For the Fatah organization, this was . . . a real revolution. Prior to the eruption of the [Second] Intifada, members of Fatah, many of whom had served in the security forces of the Palestinian Authority, had refrained from any direct involvement in terrorist activities, let alone suicide actions . . . In the first period of these events . . . veteran activists restricted themselves to shooting incidents aimed at Israeli civilian and military targets and younger members took part in heavy riots . . . However, these 'small noises' . . . got lost in the mayhem of the multitude of suicide attacks perpetrated by Hamas . . .[63]

By 2002, Fatah had managed to 'outbid' Hamas: in the first six months of the year, the Al Aqsa Brigades were responsible for more suicide bombings than all the other Palestinian terrorist groups, including Hamas, taken together.[64]

Similar dynamics could be observed in post-invasion Iraq, especially during the civil war phase from early 2006 to early 2008, when attacks on civilians by terrorist and insurgent groups were widespread. The conflict that took place at the time was fought on several fronts – against Coalition forces, the Iraqi government and its security agencies, between different ethnic groups and militias, as well as among them – and it would be ridiculous to attribute all, or even most, of the violence employed during that period to intra-sectarian competition and outbidding. At the same time, it seems plausible that, given the large number of competing violent actors on all sides, outbidding played *some* role in fuelling the conflict. For instance, even the most cursory reading of the literature about the fractured Sunni insurgent movement makes it clear that Al Qaeda in Iraq's brutal campaign of suicide bombings was setting the pace for other Sunni groups, and that the idea of outbidding was underlying their respective decisions to escalate.[65]

In fact, outbidding and competition also appear to explain the Shia militias' campaigns. The academic Michael Boyle produced a sober statistical analysis of civilian deaths in each of the country's regions and matched them with the number of armed actors.[66] What he found was that the greatest number of deaths occurred in places that contained sectarian interfaces and mixed populations, such as Baghdad, which makes any differentiation between 'genuine' sectarian hatred and intra-group violence difficult. However, he also discovered that 'a surprisingly large proportion of violence' against civilians happened in regions of the country that had no obvious significance in the inter-sectarian confrontation at all. This, he argued, confirmed 'anecdotal reports from regions like Basra that the major competition for power is between Shi'a sectarian militias, not between the major sectarian groups'.[67]

The 'CNN effect' in reverse

Some of the processes specifically associated with globalization have fuelled the developments described above. For example, the proliferation of satellite television, information technology and people's near-instantaneous access to gruelling video footage from even the remotest conflict zones – often shot by the terrorists themselves – means that terrorists are now competing for attention not only with their domestic rivals or the government but with other terrorist groups from different countries with different cultural norms and different thresholds for what constitutes acceptable levels of violence. In relatively peaceful countries like Sweden or Switzerland, a single murder might have been sufficient to grab an audience's attention in the past. In the current era, the proliferation of extreme violence via the media may compel domestic terrorists to embrace mass-casualty attacks or engage in extreme brutality simply to match their audience's expectation of what 'terrorism' is about.

Scholars in the field of 'terrorism studies' have long debated the so-called 'contagion effect', that is, the idea that terrorists watch and learn from each other.[68] Yet, what can be witnessed in the present period goes far beyond the idea of

terrorist groups copying each other's tactics and should –
perhaps more accurately – be described as the 'CNN effect'
in reverse. Coined at the time of the western intervention in
Somalia in 1992, the idea of the CNN effect was that western
audiences were more likely to support (or even demand)
military interventions in foreign lands because they could see
people's suffering in real time on satellite television.[69] Many
liberal interventionists regarded the CNN effect as a positive
development because it provided a new instrument through
which to get western publics and, by extension, their governments interested in humanitarian catastrophes and political
abuses in regions which had previously been ignored.[70] What
they failed to recognize was that, if channels like CNN made
the plight of starving Somalis more relevant and pressing to
western audiences, it also confronted them with the shocking brutality of mutilated bodies, mass-casualty attacks and
beheadings. No matter how 'civilized' a country's culture of
debate and conflict, the CNN effect introduced new audiences
– ordinary people as well as potential terrorists – to the nasti-
ness of global politics, and it primed their sense of what level
of violence was required in order to 'get through'.

Take, for example, some of the recent terrorist plots in
Britain. In 2007, a group of British Al Qaeda supporters from
Birmingham were planning to abduct a Muslim soldier in the
British army, make him demand the withdrawal of British
troops from Afghanistan and – then – behead him. Inspired
by the gruesome tactics of the former leader of Al Qaeda in
Iraq, Abu Musab al Zarqawi, the aim was to deter Muslims
from joining the British army. Filming was considered essential: one of the web sites, which the plotters had accessed in
preparation for the kidnap, advised them to 'video the operation so that it can have a bigger set of viewers and can be used
by the media'.[71] The beheading itself was to be carried out in
the most grotesquely brutal fashion possible. The group's

ringleader instructed one of his followers to 'cut [the head] off like you cut a pig, man'.[72]

A similar instance of 'CNN in reverse' was the attack on Glasgow airport in July of the same year. Carried out by a group of foreign-born doctors, the attackers' intention was to drive a Jeep Cherokee packed with gas canisters into the entrance hall of the airport and cause an explosion. The similarity between the attack and the frequent use of so-called 'vehicle-borne explosive devices' (VED) in Iraq was immediately noted by many commentators. Indeed, it later transpired that the leader of the group had been 'obsessed with the Iraq war'[73] and had seen hundreds of Internet video clips of explosions exactly like the one that was intended in Glasgow.[74]

However, the most significant example of the kind of 'contagion' which has become commonplace in the era of new terrorism is the advent of suicide terrorism in Afghanistan. Needless to say, Afghanistan has a long history of bitter and often brutal conflict, yet suicide terrorism had neither been used in the fight against the Soviet occupation in the 1980s (see chapter 4), nor was it common in the period immediately after the western invasion of the country in late 2001. There had been only a handful of suicide attacks in the first three years after the invasion, all of them directed against military targets.[75] In 2005, however, there were 17 such bombings and, in 2006, the number increased to 123; in 2007 it reached 160.[76] The rise of the tactic came as a surprise because suicide attacks, especially those directed at civilian targets, were regarded as alien to local culture and customs, and even radical leaders had spoken out strongly against them, refuting the idea that attackers should be considered as 'martyrs'.[77] In fact, when the first attacks against civilian targets occurred, Afghanis considered it inconceivable that locals could have been involved. No doubt, some face-to-face contacts with terrorists in Pakistan and virtual learning through the Internet had helped in transferring the know-how for conducting suicide bombing campaigns.[78] Equally, though, many experts believe that the sudden appearance of suicide bombings had much to do with the example set by the insurgency in Iraq and the consequent change of what was deemed acceptable and/or required in order to 'get through' to television audiences, especially in the West, gain attention and, thus, achieve strategic effects.[79]

In this chapter, it was shown that the trend towards greater brutality and lethality in new terrorism is a product of the forces which have unfolded in the age of late modernity and globalization. On the one hand, the (new) media age has made it more difficult for terrorists to 'get through'. 'Getting through' is essential for terrorists whose strategy relies on exploiting the symbolic and communicative effects of violence. However, in an era in which audiences have become desensitized to seeing violence on their television screens and media usage has become more diversified, the threshold for what is considered shocking or terrifying has risen so that ever more gruesome and deadly attacks are necessary in order to reach people and affect their behaviour. Furthermore, international competition and 'contagion' have levelled the expectations of what degree of violence is needed in order to 'get through', producing a CNN effect in reverse whereby images of terrorist atrocities overseas are priming people's expectations of what terrorism constitutes and what level of violence and type of attack to expect at home. Indeed, the new media environment, together with other developments described in this chapter, has intensified well-established terrorist dynamics such as outbidding, leading to higher casualty rates and more deadly attacks. In addition, it is worth noting that – in some cases – the difficulty in getting through has prompted terrorists to embrace alternative strategies, such as deploying 'unusual' suicide bombers who attract attention because of their unconventional profile and/or background.

The trend towards greater brutality and lethality has been underpinned by changes in ideology that have come about as a result of the 'crisis' of late modernity, globalization and the end of the Cold War. Most of the 'terrorism studies' literature focuses on the rise of religiously inspired ideologies, but the more significant, overarching development has been the decline of universalist ideologies and their gradual replacement with particularist ideas. Religiously inspired ideologies are one part of this trend, but an overly narrow focus on religion fails to account for the continued strength of nationalism, ethnicity and other 'identity ideologies' that are underlying terrorist campaigns in many parts of the world. In fact, the various examples cited in this chapter demonstrate that it was the difference between particularism and universalism – not just between religious and secular – which constituted the significant variable that explained a group's willingness to target civilians and engage in 'collective revenge' against individuals or groups of individuals that were considered to represent the 'other'. While left-wing ideologies in particular may not have prevented such targeting altogether, they nevertheless served as a restraint which may have contributed to avoiding excesses and to making terrorists 'think twice' about targeting individuals who could also be 'workers' and 'comrades'. Indeed, it was also shown that the rise of particularism can play an important role in processes like outbidding by raising the overall threshold for what is considered a necessary level of violence and, thus, forcing universalist groups to adapt their tactics accordingly.

However, saying that the late modern era has produced the trend towards greater lethality and brutality does not mean that this trend is open-ended and unlimited. Throughout this work, it was emphasized that nearly all terrorist groups – even those of the supposedly nihilist variety, such as Al Qaeda – have a constituency to which they are responsive to varying degrees. They also need to be watchful of their adversaries who, in most cases, are larger and more powerful and possess the ability to 'crack down' on them ruthlessly if they consider the terrorist group an existential threat and think there is a public consensus for doing so. In an earlier work, Mike Smith and I constructed the notion of the 'escalation trap' to describe the situation in which escalating levels of violence – that is, mass-casualty attacks and greater brutality – are necessary in order for terrorists to 'get through' and achieve strategic effects but which, simultaneously, lead to a public backlash that alienates the terrorists from their constituency and enables the authorities to take harsh and repressive measures to destroy the group.[80] There may be a ceiling, therefore, at which ever greater lethality and brutality become counterproductive and, rather than improving the terrorists' chances of success, diminish them.

In Egypt, for example, the 'escalation trap' led to the destruction of Gamaat Islamiya (Islamic Group) in the mid-1990s. In 1992, the Islamic Group launched a terrorist campaign against targets related to the tourism industry. Not only was the killing of non-Muslim foreigners permitted from an ideological point of view, it also promised to undermine one of the main sources of revenue for the Egyptian state. In reality, though, the campaign turned the population against the terrorists. There was a genuine outcry, for instance, when the group killed 18 Greek tourists (who were mistaken for Israelis) in 1996. Moreover, the campaign affected not only the Egyptian state but, more importantly, hundreds of thousands of ordinary Egyptians whose livelihoods depended on the tourism industry. As a result, the Islamic Group came to be isolated even among Islamist sympathizers, which meant that the government encountered little opposition when implementing some of its harshest counter-terrorism policies. By 1997, when a dissident faction decided to attempt 'one last push' by massacring nearly 60 (mostly Swiss) tourists in Luxor, most of the group, including its leadership, were behind bars and even in radical circles the campaign was regarded with disgust.[81]

A similar scenario may currently be unfolding in the case of Al Qaeda. As explained in this chapter, even some of the most loyal and committed followers of the group have come to question the wisdom of the campaign and the results it has produced. There is a genuine debate within the broader Al Qaeda movement about the use of indiscriminate tactics. This may not yet amount to a complete switch from particularism to universalism, as most of the criticism appears to be geared towards Al Qaeda's killing of other Muslims rather than non-Muslims. But it seems clear that the group's leadership is, for the first time since the September 11 attacks against the United States, on the defensive. And indeed, there seem to be voices within the wider movement who go even further and condemn the targeting of civilians outright. Whether Al Qaeda has already fallen into the 'escalation trap' is difficult to tell, especially when considering that overly indiscriminate actions against Muslim civilians by western powers could – once again – legitimate Al Qaeda in the eyes of its followers. More broadly, though, the case of Al Qaeda is a good example of how even a supposedly nihilist terrorist group does not exist in a political and societal vacuum but is responsive to a constituency and its demands as well as broader political dynamics. Even for particularist organizations in the era of new terrorism, therefore, there may be limits at which the push towards greater lethality and brutality can become negative. What this means for counter-terrorism policy will be explored in the concluding chapter.

CHAPTER SIX

Confronting the New Terrorism

Part of the impetus for writing this book came from the frustration with the academic field of 'terrorism studies' which often perceives terrorism as something that can be studied in isolation from broader socio-political trends and developments. In reality, of course, it is essential to study and understand the political, economic and social forces that have shaped society and/or a particular period because terrorism – like everything else – is one of their expressions. Only such a rigorous and holistic approach can prevent muddled thinking and confused ideas. Take, for example, the widespread view that the September 11 attacks against the United States were a contradiction of globalization. The opposite is true. There could not have been a more complete expression of globalization than a transnational terrorist group producing a terrorist 'spectacular' for the benefit of television viewers across the world. Indeed, the September 11 attacks made it clear that global terrorists are part of globalization as much as global markets are.

What, then, is the new terrorism, and where did it come from? The first and perhaps most fundamental assumption underlying everything that has been said about the phenomenon is that new terrorism still constitutes terrorism. Some of the critics of the concept seem to think that, for new terrorism to be considered genuinely 'new', it needs to have mutated into something completely different.[1] Yet, like old terrorism, it consists of symbolic acts of violence carried out for political purposes by small, conspiratorial groups. Rather than creating entirely different categories, new terrorism should – and indeed must – be understood as the sum of all the changes that have occurred within these variables.

Second, new terrorism did not emerge overnight and it would be mistaken to think of its rise in terms of a clean, easily identifiable break with the old. There is no clear-cut juncture nor is there a 'starting date'. In fact, it would be misleading to conceptualize the new terrorism in relation to 'before' and 'after' because it has resulted from trends and developments that have started at different points and evolved over a considerable period of time. Some of them arose separately, but they all have their roots in late modernity and its most novel manifestation, globalization. For example, the networking and transnationalization of terrorism, which were described in chapter 3, have largely been driven by the rise of cheap international travel and information technology, both of which only became mass phenomena in the early 1990s and – especially in the case of the Internet – may not even be close to having unleashed their full potential. By contrast, the religious revival and, more specifically, the rise of religiously inspired political ideologies, which were explored in chapter 4, have their roots in the dialectic of (late) modernity and have come to the fore since the late 1970s. On the other hand, the increases in lethality and brutality, which constitute a third defining feature of new terrorism and were discussed in chapter 5, are even more difficult to pinpoint because they draw on a combination of the different drivers and 'root causes' described above, in particular the rise of identity ideologies (of which religion is one) and the impact of new forms of media.

A third point worth keeping in mind is that there is no single terrorist group that would perfectly combine all the different characteristics of new terrorism. Many analyses of the new terrorism derive the concept from just one of its empirical manifestations instead of constructing a conceptual framework which can be tested in different cases. In other words, for many authors, new terrorism is synonymous with Al Qaeda and, in some cases, it seems that the whole empirical basis for the hypothesis is just one event, that is, the September 11 attacks against the United States.[2] Such a narrow approach leads to significant distortions. As explained in chapter 2, Al Qaeda comes close to matching the new terrorism model – it is transnational, religiously inspired and engages in mass-casualty attacks – which explains why many references and examples in this book are drawn from its activities and evolution. But, as chapter 3 showed, there are groups other than Al Qaeda whose organizational model fits the idea of 'leaderless resistance' even better. The Earth Liberation Front (ELF), for instance, may neither be religiously motivated nor carry out mass-casualty attacks but it is truly leaderless – held together merely by a web site and a common ideology.

At what point, then, does a terrorist group become 'new'? How many of the characteristics of the new terrorism are required for the label to be justified? It seems obvious that new terrorism must not be used as a static concept, nor should analysts be fixated by the activities of one terrorist group alone. Rather, as this book has shown, new terrorism is best understood as a methodology through which to systematize the process of evolutionary change, and it is more appropriate to speak of 'older' and 'newer' instead of 'old' and 'new' terrorism. Thus defined, the concept of new terrorism can be helpful in making sense of how terrorism has changed and, to some extent, in forecasting what lies ahead. Indeed, the very last section of the chapter will provide some informed speculation about the future of terrorism. First, though, it will be shown how the insights generated in this book can help in countering the evolving threat.

What needs to be done?

In drawing up a set of policy recommendations, it is neither feasible nor necessary to develop an entirely new theory of counter-terrorism because many of the long-established principles of counter-terrorism remain valid. Regardless of whether governments are dealing with 'old' or 'new', the aim must be to prevent terrorist attacks whilst maintaining legitimacy in the eyes of the population.[3] In doing so, governments need to 'harden' potential targets;[4] develop good intelligence in order to disrupt terrorist structures; bring to bear the full force of the law whilst acting within the law; address legitimate grievances where they can be addressed; and convey a sense of calm and determination when communicating with the public.[5] Any supposedly new theory would merely be a variation of these themes. What this section concentrates on, therefore, is not so much new principles of counter-terrorism but, rather, the policy areas that have been affected by the rise of the new terrorism and where changes in emphasis and approach may be necessary.

Structure and organization

One of the most significant changes associated with the rise of the new terrorism is the 'networking' of terrorist organizations. This – seemingly straightforward – development is not only not acted upon but frequently misunderstood by governments who assume that their terrorist adversaries continue to be organized in ways similar to themselves. The American scholar Marc Sageman deserves credit for raising the profile of social network analysis in the study of terrorism and, by extension, for promoting its application among law enforcement and intelligence agencies across the world.[6] Social network analysis ignores formal hierarchies and instead focuses on mapping individuals' social relationships. What emerges is a much clearer picture of who really matters within an organization. As explained in chapter 2, each network is likely to contain a number of so-called 'hubs' that may not represent the most important people in a formal sense but the 'human glue' that holds a network together. In the era of new terrorism, security agencies clearly need to focus on hubs rather than formal leaders. In fact, had the Israeli authorities utilized this methodology, perhaps their policy of targeted killings during the Second Intifada could have been more effective and less controversial. Instead of 'taking out' the political leaders of terrorist groups, they could have focused on the operational hubs that were responsible for deploying suicide bombers to Israel. That way, they would have disrupted their adversaries' activities while avoiding much of the international outcry.[7]

Another implication is the need for governments' own structures to become more adaptive and flexible. As the two analysts David Ronfeldt and John Arquilla put it, 'it takes networks to fight networks'.[8] This, of course, is easier said than done. Getting thousands – in some cases, hundreds of thousands – of people in different agencies and locations with different missions and organizational cultures to act like a network, communicate effectively and share information can be a daunting challenge. Equally, it is not easy, nor is it always desirable, to abandon long-established principles of hierarchy and promotion that have been fundamental to the organization of public service institutions for centuries. And indeed, what Ronfeldt and Arquilla are trying to suggest is not for governments to mirror their adversaries' structures but – rather – to be more willing to innovate and create new avenues for cooperation. Since the September 11 attacks in 2001, some progress has been made. In Western Europe, many intelligence agencies have opened up, doing away with much of the unnecessary secrecy that had hindered effective communication with other agencies and the outside world. So-called 'fusion centres' – such as the Joint Terrorism Analysis Centre (JJAC) in Britain or the National Counterterrorism Center (NCTC) in the United States – in which government agencies are pooling their information on issues such as terrorism have sprung up everywhere, giving rise to a new spirit of cooperation regardless of individuals' institutional affiliations or bureaucratic rank. These are positive signs but it will require continued effort as well as constant evaluation and the sharing of best practices in order for governments to maintain an edge over their terrorist adversaries.

International cooperation

A second area in which the rise of the new terrorism has presented governments with new challenges is that of international cooperation. Governments embody the principle of national sovereignty, and everything they do is organized accordingly. The separation between internal and external – between domestic and foreign – is critical to their functioning. Arguably, it represents their *raison d'être*, and terrorists, even in the era of old terrorism, have exploited this. One of the key factors in terrorist and guerrilla campaigns throughout the twentieth century was the availability of a porous international border that could be crossed in order to escape a hostile government's reach. This helped the Algerian National Liberation Front (FLN) in their country's war of independence as much as it aided the IRA in its thirty-year long confrontation with the British government. There is nothing new, therefore, in calling for more international cooperation, but the call has become more urgent with the rise of transnational terrorism. Whereas the number of jurisdictions involved in IRA investigations rarely exceeded three (typically the UK, the Republic of Ireland and sometimes another European country or the United States), Al Qaeda-related cases routinely involve up to ten different countries. In fact, not only is there a larger number of countries to deal with, the countries are more distant and in many cases there are no pre-existing relationships between the relevant security agencies.[9] In other words, the era of new terrorism requires more – as well as more demanding – interaction with foreign countries.

Unfortunately, there are few areas in which intergovernmental relations are more fraught with difficulty than counter-terrorism. At the political level, one of the most fundamental problems impeding more comprehensive and institutionalized cooperation is the lack of a common understanding of what constitutes terrorism. Even if an international consensus could be achieved, some countries may still be hesitant to share sensitive information with countries that are seen as hostile, while others will be reluctant to receive intelligence from governments that are known to engage in human rights abuses. At the practical level, all cooperation requires trust. Trust, however, emerges only when individuals have the opportunity to get to know and interact with each other. Given the number of countries, geographical distances and foreign languages involved in countering the new terrorism, this represents a greater hurdle than in previous historical periods. Some idealists may dream of creating a multilateral institution through which all this could be facilitated. In reality, such a model would not even work within the European Union – despite European countries' successful cooperation in other areas and their exceptionally close political and cultural ties. As a result, even the United Nations have come to recognize that, for the foreseeable future, international cooperation on counter-terrorism issues will continue to rely on informal, ad hoc forums that involve mostly bilateral contacts.[10] This makes the process of building trust and cooperation across borders seem messy and slow but no less important.

Messaging

A recurring theme has been terrorists' use of information technology as a means of maintaining their movement, influencing their constituency and popularizing their cause. This is an area in which governments have been remarkably passive. As a first – albeit fundamentally important – step, it will be critical for governments to understand quite how significant messaging and the new media have become. Terrorists' use of the new media has long evolved beyond the release of video messages on *Al Jazeera*. In Iraq and Afghanistan, the insurgents are filming every operation, with professionally produced 'snuff movies' likely to be posted on the Internet hours before any reporters arrive on the scene.[11] By contrast, and despite spending hundreds of millions on press officers and media operations, western governments are still underrepresented in cyber space. Ministers may be announcing road shows and other token initiatives as a way of wooing 'vulnerable youth' but they have completely failed to engage in the proverbial battle for hearts and minds in the kinds of (virtual) spaces in which today's young people socialize, exchange views and from which they receive much of their information about the world.

Upon realizing that 'bad things' happen on the Internet, most governments' instinctive response is to call for the banning of certain web sites or content. And indeed, there may be occasions on which particularly hateful, offensive or violent web sites should be taken down. But – as the Irish analyst Johnny Ryan and others have shown – it would be an illusion to believe that governments can 'ban' their way out of this calamity.[12] Not only does the decentralized, global structure of the Internet make it virtually impossible to remove particular types of content for long,[13] the volume of 'radical' and 'extremist' material that is currently available would necessitate a truly Orwellian structure to ensure complete control over what can be accessed. The (uncomfortable) truth is that, instead of responding with repressive measures, governments need to become better than their terrorist adversaries at communicating their message through the Internet. Only recently have western governments started to marshal the resources of public relations and public diplomacy professionals as well as some of the brightest minds in the new media to craft an appealing message, identify target audiences and engage with them. Yet there are few areas in which governments' systematic engagement and sustained efforts are of greater strategic importance. Terrorist adversaries come and go, but the new media and the Internet are here to stay.

Counter-ideology

A final area in which the new terrorism may require new kinds of responses is that of counter-ideology. The standard liberal response to the rise of identity ideologies is to invoke the virtues of 'cosmopolitanism'.[14] There are different varieties of the concept[15] but they all share the same basic idea, namely the need to overcome national, ethnic and religious boundaries and identities by promoting a shared sense of humanity, universal human rights and inclusive forms of democracy. Traditionally, cosmopolitanism's main foe has been nationalism but, in principle, it is opposed to all forms of exclusiveness and particularism, including religiously inspired political ideologies. In its purest form, then, it aims at no less than eliminating the opposition between 'us' and 'them' which – in the eyes of cosmopolitans – has caused most conflicts and, in the context of terrorism, makes it possible to target civilian populations as a form of punishing entire nations, or ethnic or religious groups. If everyone believed in cosmopolitan ideas – so the argument goes – particularist terrorism would have nowhere to go.

At first, the argument seems compelling but it becomes less so when one considers the context and circumstances in which some of the 'identity ideologies' that form part of the new terrorism have arisen. As explained in chapter 4, the religious revival and its subsequent transformation into religiously inspired political ideologies occurred *precisely because* people had been overwhelmed by universalizing influences and were seeking to reassert a sense of belonging. In other words, it was the aggressive promotion of universal values through the forces of late modernity and globalization that provoked the revival of identity. If this is true, what hope is there that the forceful promotion of yet another form of modernizing universalism – cosmopolitanism – will solve the problem? As recent decades have shown, people have a natural longing for identity, especially in periods of great change in which a sense of fragility and uncertainty is all-pervasive. Rather than telling people that identity – whether religious, ethnic, national or otherwise – is 'bad' and must be overcome, the more promising way forward would be to focus on encouraging soft, inclusive identities which recognize differences and teach people how to deal with them.

Meanwhile, some followers of the cosmopolitan school have recognized the importance of identity and formulated new concepts such as 'rooted cosmopolitanism' which would allow people to express some degree of belonging after all.[16] However well intentioned, such efforts will do little to correct the basic flaws of the concept. As the former Soviet dissident Natan Sharanksy put it:

> In the end, all these types of rooted cosmopolitanism, or 'progressive' and acceptable nationalisms, come to one thing: The good nationalist is the one who is ready to give up his nationalism, the one for whom nationalism is unimportant . . . You can enjoy nationalism as a kind of decoration, like going to a museum and appreciating all the different forms of art, or going to a festival and tasting the wide variety of ethnic foods. But real life, we are told, should be expressed

not in these differences but rather in . . . [a] dedication to a
world of human rights without conflict.[17]

Indeed, clinging to the utopia of cosmopolitanism will only
make it more difficult for societies to accept identity and learn
to deal with it in more productive ways.

For governments, the strategic objectives are twofold. First,
they need to promote non-violent forms of expressing any
identity or ideology, because challenging the particular mode
through which grievances are expressed will always be less
complicated than arguing with the grievances themselves.
Hence, similar to the way in which international norms
against slavery and genocide have gradually taken hold,
there may be value in promoting norms which consider the
targeting of civilians through mass-casualty attacks as unac-
ceptable.[18] In parallel, publics should be educated about the
ineffectiveness of terrorist violence which, as recent surveys
have shown, is spectacularly unsuccessful in achieving its
stated objectives,[19] especially when compared to other forms
of waging conflict, such as civil resistance and non-violent
strategic action.[20] These types of arguments may not appeal to
existentialists in the vein of Frantz Fanon who believe that the
shedding of blood has a cathartic effect.[21] But for most potential terrorists – even religiously inspired ones – knowing that
one's sacrifice will make a difference to their cause is essential
to justifying their involvement.

A second objective is to soften the particularist ideologies that
are underlying the new terrorism, so that the killing of innocent
people based merely on their ethnic or religious community
becomes inconceivable. A good example of how particularist
ideologies can be softened can be found in the many European
countries that are currently undergoing a process of redefining
their national identities. Long based on monocultural and particularist ideas, the waves of immigration that have taken place

in the post-war period have forced these countries to think again about the essence of being British, German, French and so on, reformulating concepts like integration and citizenship to allow for more inclusive expressions. This shows that, over time, even strongly particularist narratives can be refined to accommodate more universalist ideas. But it also highlights the importance of not doing away with identity altogether. Unless identities such as 'being British' or 'being German' have meaning – unless, in other words, they go beyond national folklore and ethnic food and provide a real sense of belonging and distinctiveness – people will fail to see the point in taking concepts such as citizenship and community seriously. In fact, the more traditional identities get hollowed out, the more likely people are to look for alternative providers of meaning and certainty, including fundamentalist religion and other particularist narratives. Indeed, of all the challenges presented in this section, finding the right balance between universalism and identity will undoubtedly remain the most difficult yet most frequently recurring question in the era of late modernity and globalization.

What lies ahead?

Forecasting is not as easy as drawing a straight line, assuming that existing trends will remain important and continue uninterrupted. Just because information technology has made transnational terrorist networks possible does not mean that every terrorist group will become a form of globalized leaderless resistance. Just because religion has come to play a greater role does not mean that other ideologies will be completely marginalized. And just because terrorist incidents produce more casualties does not mean that there is no limit at all. It may not be possible, therefore, to predict the future based merely on what is known about the past. Nevertheless, some of the dynamics and processes that have been identified in this book allow for a number of meaningful statements about what lies ahead.

Terrorism is rooted in the real world and, more specifically, the political cleavages that exist in societies or, increasingly, at the global level. If the aim is to predict what kinds of ideas and ideologies the terrorists of the future will be motivated by, it is important, therefore, to begin by looking at the evolution of radical movements and all the political discourses that exist on the fringes of the mainstream. Terrorist groups evolve out of broader political movements and it is by looking at these movements – their ideas, narratives and internal dynamics, as well as their changing attitudes towards political participation – that one can learn most about the future of terrorism. Terrorism, after all, is a form of political violence: to understand where the next terrorist 'wave' will come from, one needs to be good at picking up on social trends and political ideas, not just at interpreting their violent expressions.

Being political implies, furthermore, that terrorism is not limitless. While, by definition, it is meant to shock and 'terrorize', it is also directed at an internal audience which terrorist groups hope to influence and incite. Even religiously inspired movements have a constituency in the real world whose continued support and positive response is as important to them as what they imagine to be the word of God. No doubt, killing plenty of innocent civilians can be popular as long as they represent the 'other'. As shown in the previous chapter, during the Second Intifada, large segments of the Palestinian population approved of suicide missions against soft Israeli targets, and Hamas's willingness to satisfy that demand played an important role in its rise to prominence. No doubt, also, the threshold for gaining attention has risen. At the same time, there continues to be a ceiling at which excessive violence becomes counterproductive by 'turning off' part of the terrorists' constituency and inviting massive retaliation.

One may argue, of course, that this 'moderating' influence is counteracted by the transnationalization and networking of terrorism which makes constituencies less tangible and empowers grassroots followers at the expense of the more far-sighted, strategically oriented leaders who used to be the ones that were in control of a campaign. Teenage 'bunches of guys' – to use Sageman's expression – will not have the same awareness of a movement's wider objectives or the views of its constituency. Lacking any rational strategy for achieving political change, their actions may be driven purely by a sense of rage and thus be without any constraint. At the same time, if truly leaderless, they will lack the resources and skills that are needed to translate ideas into effective action. Their terrorism – however limitless their intentions – will end up being fairly limited in its consequences.

It may be reasonable to 'predict', therefore, that the greatest future danger will come neither from highly disciplined organizations with strong constituencies and a high degree of political awareness nor from the truly leaderless resisters. Rather, the greatest risks are most likely to emanate from those who are semi-linked into more structured networks, having obtained training, resources and skills, but who refuse to subject themselves to their discipline and strategic direction.

What makes this (and similar) forecasts risky is that no one quite knows how events will interfere with the careful and systematic application of insights based on long-term trends. As mentioned in chapter 4, prior to the September 11 attacks, many of the most distinguished experts in the field had predicted the decline of radical Islam. This shows that one simply cannot tell what kind of 'game-changing' events lie ahead and how exactly they will play out. The word 'prediction' should therefore be used with great caution, especially when considering the forecasts of future sources of terrorism which are given in the following.

Based on the trends and developments that have been discussed in previous chapters, it seems clear that – in addition to the revival of identity ideologies more generally – two radical political movements that have sprung up as a direct consequence, and in opposition to, globalization may soon resort to terrorist means.[22] One – the so-called anti-globalization movement – is universalist in character and believes that the kind of globalization that is currently unfolding is a mere continuation of imperialist practices whereby the political and economic elites in the 'Global North' impose neo-liberal, exploitative practices on the 'Global South'. Arguably, radical environmentalists (who are considered part of this movement) have had no qualms about breaking the law and, on several occasions, have used acts of violence to get their message across. Indeed, leaderless and decentralized groups such as the ELF (see chapter 3, pp. 65–7) are prototypes for the type of terrorism that could emerge. However, given their universalist orientation, it seems highly unlikely that such groups would resort to mass-casualty attacks against civilians.

The other movement that has gained strength in response to the pressures from globalization is the anti-immigrant Right across Western Europe and North America. Like the anti-globalization movement, it opposes neo-liberal economic policies, especially the liberalization of trade and immigration, but it does so from a particularist perspective. Their constituency consists of globalization 'losers' in the West, that is, unskilled workers and those on low incomes who have been exposed to increased competition and feel that their identity as well as their livelihoods are under threat from immigrants and other foreign influences. So far, the movement has largely manifested itself in the rise of populist right-wing parties in Western Europe who have successfully competed in elections in countries like Belgium, Austria and France, but there has also been a significant rise in the number of incidents in violent attacks. There are frequent and ongoing discussions among neo-Nazis about the establishment of 'Brown Army Factions'[23] similar to the old left-wing terrorist groups in the 1970s and 1980s. The right-wing extremist movement is highly networked already, and these structures would consequently be reflected in any terrorist group to emerge from the movement. Considering their particularist ideas, the repertoire of tactics is likely to include not only assassinations of, say, prominent public figures of foreign, Muslim or Jewish descent but also attacks against soft targets, such as mosques, synagogues and immigration centres.

The jihadist movement, on the other hand, appears to have reached a critical juncture, and it is impossible to make any precise forecasts when the picture is as confusing and contradictory as it seems right now. As a radical political movement, Islamism continues to attract a substantial following but support for terrorism has declined, not least because of the actions of terrorist groups like Al Qaeda. It may well be correct to argue that Al Qaeda has fallen into the 'escalation trap' from which it will be difficult to recover. Despite having expanded their base in the tribal areas of Pakistan, the movement has faced a public backlash in nearly all of the 'central theatres' in which it had hoped to gain traction.[24] At the same time, the grievances on which its campaign has rested continue to exist, and some of the territorially based groups like Hezbollah and Hamas, which regardless of their differences also draw on the canon of beliefs that underlie radical Islam, continue to prosper. It is definitely too soon, therefore, to predict – yet again – the decline of radical Islam, nor would it be appropriate to say that the age of Islamist terrorism has come to a close. But it is worth noting that those groups who combine radical Islam with a local, nationalist agenda have survived better than the transnational project embodied by Al

Qaeda.[25] Perhaps, this is evidence that, even in the age of globalization, nationalism and national roots still matter.

Of course, there always remains the risk of catastrophic or apocalyptic terrorism carried out by sectarian or millenarian cults with little or no political agenda at all. This risk, however, is not new nor is it very substantial. Walter Laqueur's idea – mentioned at the very beginning of this book – that terrorists will operate earthquake machines and launch artificial meteors in order to 'liquidate all satanic forces [and destroy] all life on earth'[26] has no basis in fact. Such predictions are science fiction and will remain just that. This is not to trivialize the danger or, more importantly, its potential consequences. In an era in which borders have become porous and information technology has enabled unprecedented global levels of exchange, inevitably the risk of terrorists acquiring chemical, biological, nuclear or radiological materials has increased. Policy makers are right in taking every measure possible to avert it. More generally, though, there is nothing to suggest that apocalyptic terrorism constitutes a 'trend' based on anything we have seen or observed in the past few decades. The new terrorism is more lethal and in many ways more dangerous than its predecessor. But, to paraphrase Mark Twain, reports about the end of the world have been greatly exaggerated.

Notes

CHAPTER 1 INTRODUCTION

1 Walter Laqueur, *The New Terrorism: Fanaticism and the Arms of Mass Destruction* (Oxford: Oxford University Press, 1999), p. 81.

2 Ibid., p. 264.

3 Walter Laqueur, 'Postmodern Terrorism: New Rules for an Old Game', *Foreign Affairs*, 75(5) 1996; available at http://www.foreignaffairs.org/19960901faessay4222/walter-laqueur/postmodern-terrorism-new-rules-for-an-old-game.html.

4 Most of the contributors to the original debate about the 'new' terrorism in the 1990s are cited in this chapter. Recently, however, there has been a revival of some of these debates. See, for example, Brian M. Jenkins, *Will Terrorists Go Nuclear?* (New York: Prometheus, 2008); Thomas Mockaitis, *The 'New' Terrorism: Myths and Reality* (Stanford, CA: Stanford Security Press, 2008). Undoubtedly the most important recent contribution to the debate is Philip Bobbitt, *Terror and Consent: The Wars for the Twenty-First Century* (New York: Knopf, 2008).

5 'RAF-Auflösungserklärung', released in March 1998; available at http://www.rafinfo.de/archiv/raf/raf-20-4-98.php.

6 See Daniel Benjamin and Steven Simon, *The Age of Sacred Terror* (New York: Random House, 2002), pp. 6–11.

7 See David E. Kaplan, 'Aum Shinrikyo (1995)', in Jonathan B. Tucker (ed.), *Toxic Terror: Assessing Terrorist Use of Chemical and Biological Weapons* (Cambridge, MA: MIT Press, 2000), pp. 210–13.

8 See, for example, Ehud Sprinzak, 'The Great Superterrorism Scare', *Foreign Policy*, Autumn 1998, pp. 110–23; Francois Heisbourg, *Hyperterrorisme: la nouvelle guerre* (Paris: Odile Jacob, 2001); Paul Schulte, 'Uncertain Diagnosis: Megalomaniacal Hyper-Terrorism and an Unending War for the Future', in David

Martin Jones (ed.), *Globalisation and the New Terror: The Asia Pacific Dimension* (Cheltenham: Edward Elgar, 2004), pp. 29–39.

9 For some of the more interesting contributions, see 'America and the New Terrorism: An Exchange', *Survival*, 42(2) (2000): 156–72, 417–28; Brian Michael Jenkins, 'Terrorism and Beyond: A 21st Century Perspective', *Studies in Conflict and Terrorism*, 24 (2001): 321–7; Ian O. Lesser et al. (eds), *Countering the New Terrorism* (Santa Monica: RAND, 1999); Steven Simon and Daniel Benjamin, 'America and the New Terrorism', *Survival*, 42(1) (2000).

10 As Mike Smith and I have shown, 'terrorism studies' may not even be a particularly good tool for predicting the dynamics of violence which unfold in campaigns of terror. See Peter R. Neumann and M. L. R. Smith, *The Strategy of Terrorism* (London: Routledge, 2007), ch. 6.

11 See, for example, Bruce Hoffman, 'Terrorism Trends and Prospects' in ibid., ch. 2.

12 Brian Michael Jenkins, 'Foreword' in Lesser, *Countering the New Terrorism*, p. viii.

13 See, for example, Benjamin R. Barber, *Jihad vs. McWorld* (New York: Ballantine, 1995).

14 In the late 1980s, the two academics Alex Schmid and Albert Jongman conducted an extensive survey, which concluded that 'violence' was the only characteristic of terrorism which a clear majority could agree upon. See Alex Schmid and Albert Jongman, *Political Terrorism* (New Brunswick: Transaction Books, 1988), pp. 5–6.

15 See Alex Schmid, 'Terrorism – The Definitional Problem', *Case Western Reserve Journal of International Law*, 36(2) (2004): 399. Also Bruce Hoffman, *Inside Terrorism*, 2nd ed. (New York: Columbia University Press, 2006), ch. 2.

16 Alex Schmid, 'Terrorism': 376.

17 Neumann, *The Strategy of Terrorism*, ch. 1.

18 Ibid., p. 394. In this context, it is worth considering the work done by the United Nations' High-Level Panel on Threats, Challenges, and Change, which set the tone for Kofi Annan's later endorsements. See United Nations, *A More Secure World: Our Shared Responsibility* (New York: United Nations, 2004), pp. 51–2. Available at http://www.un.org/secureworld/report2.pdf.

19 See, for example, Christopher C. Harmon, *Terrorism Today*

(London: Frank Cass, 2000), p. 21; Jessica Stern, *The Ultimate Terrorists* (Cambridge, MA: Harvard University Press, 1999), p. 11.

20 T. P. Thornton, 'Terror as a Weapon of Political Agitation' in Harry Eckstein (ed.), *Internal War: Problems and Approaches* (New York: Free Press, 1964), pp. 73–5.

21 See also Peter Waldmann, *Terrorismus: Provokation der Macht*, 2nd ed. (Hamburg: Murmann, 2005), pp. 12–17.

22 Zygmunt Bauman, *Liquid Modernity* (Cambridge: Polity, 2000); Anthony Giddens, *The Consequences of Modernity* (Cambridge: Polity, 1990). See also Ulrich Beck, Anthony Giddens and Scott Lash, *Reflexive Modernization: Politics, Tradition and Aesthetics in the Modern Social Order* (Oxford: Blackwell, 1994).

23 Anthony Giddens, *The Consequences of Modernity*, p. 63. See also Ulrich Beck, *Weltrisikogesellschaft: Auf der Suche nach der verlorenen Sicherheit* (Frankfurt/Main: Suhrkamp, 2007), ch. 1.

24 See Paul Hirst and Grahame Thompson, *Globalization in Question* (Cambridge: Polity, 1999), ch. 2.

25 David Held and Anthony McGrew, David Goldblatt and Jonathan Perraton, 'Rethinking Globalization', in David Held and Anthony McGrew (eds), *The Global Transformations Reader*, 2nd ed. (Cambridge: Polity, 2003), pp. 67–8.

26 Ibid., p. 68.

27 David Held and Anthony McGrew, 'The Great Globalization Debate: An Introduction' in Held, *The Global Transformations Reader*, p. 4. Also Jan Aart Scholte, *Globalisation: A Critical Introduction* (Basingstoke: Palgrave, 2005), ch. 4.

28 See Manfred B. Steger, *Globalism* (New York: Rowman and Littlefield, 2002).

29 Admittedly, though, he occasionally mentions 'angry' super-empowered individuals who might become a threat to the United States. Thomas L. Friedman, *The Lexus and the Olive Tree* (New York: Farrar, Straus and Giroux, 1999), p. 381.

30 'Remarks of former US President Bill Clinton', *Harvard University Gazette*, 6 June 2007; available at http://www.news.harvard.edu/gazette/2007/06.07/99-clinton.html.

31 See Thomas Copeland, 'Is the "New Terrorism" Really New? An Analysis of the New Paradigm for Terrorism', *The Journal of Conflict Studies*, 12(2) (2001): 92–105; Isabelle Duyvesteyn, 'How New Is the New Terrorism?', *Studies in Conflict and Terrorism*, 27 (2004): 439–54; Alexander Spencer, 'Questioning the Concept

of "New Terrorism"', *Peace, Conflict and Development*, 8 (2006), http://www.peacestudiesjournal.org.uk/docs/Feb%2006%20 SPENCER%2oversion%202.pdf; David Tucker, 'What is New about the New Terrorism and How Dangerous Is It?', *Terrorism and Political Violence*, 13(3) (2001): 1–14.

32 Mary Kaldor, *New and Old Wars: Organized Violence in a Global Era* (Stanford: Stanford University Press, 1999). For a summary of the critique, see Edward Newman, 'The "New Wars" Debate: A Historical Perspective Is Needed', *Security Dialogue*, 35 (2004): 173–89.

33 Duyvesteyn, 'How New Is the New Terrorism?', p. 439. See also Waldmann, *Terrorismus*, pp. 30–1.

34 I wish to thank Christoph Neumann for this insight.

35 Thomas G. Weiss, *Humanitarian Intervention* (Cambridge: Polity, 2007), p. 63.

36 Duyvesteyn, 'How New Is the New Terrorism?', pp. 443–5.

CHAPTER 2 OLD AND NEW TERRORISM

1 'America and the New Terrorism: An Exchange', *Survival*, 42(2) (2000): 156–72, 417–28.

2 Bruce Hoffman, 'The American Perspective' in 'America and the New Terrorism: An Exchange', *Survival*, 42(2) (2000): 163.

3 This method is similar to Martha Crenshaw's methodology. See '"New" vs. "Old" Terrorism', talk given by Martha Crenshaw at the Woodrow Wilson International Center for Scholars, Washington DC, 23 May 2005; available at http://www.wilsoncenter.org/index. cfm?event_id=122918&fuseaction=events.event_summary

4 See Martha Crenshaw, 'Thoughts on Relating Terrorism to Historical Contexts', in Martha Crenshaw (ed.), *Terrorism in Context* (University Park, PA: Pennsylvania State Press, 1995), p. 4. Also Peter Waldmann, *Terrorismus: Provokation der Macht*, 2nd ed. (Hamburg: Murmann, 2005), p. 13.

5 See Peter R. Neumann and M. L. R. Smith, *The Strategy of Terrorism: How It Works, and Why It Fails* (London: Routledge, 2008).

6 See, for example, Isabelle Duyvesteyn, 'How New Is the New Terrorism?', *Studies in Conflict and Terrorism*, 27 (2004): 439–54.

7 See David Rapoport, 'Introduction' in David Rapoport (ed.), *Inside*

Terrorist Organizations, 2nd ed. (London: Frank Cass, 2001), pp. 1–12.

8 See, for example, Gus Martin, *Understanding Terrorism: Challenges, Perspectives, and Issues* (London: Sage, 2003), p. G-5.

9 Gabi Sheffer, 'Diasporas and Terrorism' in Louise Richardson, *The Roots of Terrorism* (London and New York: Routledge, 2006).

10 See Stefan Aust, *Der Baader Meinhof Komplex*, 2nd ed. (Hamburg: Hoffmann und Campe, 1997).

11 John Arquilla and David Ronfeldt, 'The Advent of Netwar', in John Arquilla and David Ronfeldt (eds), *In Athena's Camp: Preparing for Conflict in the Information Age* (Santa Monica, CA: RAND, 1997), p. 280.

12 Ibid. See also Marc Sageman, *Understanding Terror Networks* (Philadelphia, PA: University of Pennsylvania Press, 2004), pp. 139–41.

13 See Paul Joosse, 'Leaderless Resistance and Ideological Inclusion: The Case of the Earth Liberation Front', *Terrorism and Political Violence*, 19 (2007): 352–4.

14 Louis Beam, 'Leaderless Resistance', *The Seditionist*, February 1992. Available at www.louisbeam.com/leaderless.htm.

15 Ulrich Schneckener, *Transnationaler Terrorismus* (Frankfurt/Main: Suhrkamp, 2006), pp. 49–50.

16 Olivier Roy describes this process as 'deterritorialization'. See Olivier Roy, *Globalized Islam: The Search for a New Ummah* (New York: Columbia University Press, 2004), p. 18.

17 See, for example, Duyvesteyn, 'How New Is the New Terrorism?', *Studies in Conflict and Terrorism*, 27 (2004), p. 444.

18 For an account of his trial and execution, see Isaac Cronin, *Confronting Fear: A History of Terrorism* (New York: Thunder's Mouth Press, 2002), pp. 22–32.

19 See, for example, David C. Rapoport, 'The International World as Some Terrorists Have Seen It: A Look at a Century of Memoirs', in David C. Rapoport (ed.), *Inside Terrorist Organizations*, 2nd ed. (London: Frank Cass, 2001), pp. 34–8.

20 Sidney Tarrow, *The New Transnational Activism* (Cambridge: Cambridge University Press, 2005), p. 4. Tarrow also cites a number of historical examples of transnational activism. See ibid., pp. 3–4.

21 Leonard Weinberg, 'Turning to Terror: The Conditions under

Which Political Parties Turn to Terrorist Activities', *Comparative Politics*, 23(4) (1991), pp. 431–3.

22 See Bruce Hoffman, *Inside Terrorism*, 2nd ed. (New York: Columbia University Press, 2006), ch. 2. Also David C. Rapoport, 'The Four Waves of Rebel Terror and September 11', *Anthropoetics*, 8(1) (2002); available at www.anthropoetics.ucla. edu/apo801/terror.htm.

23 The one significant exception from the dominant pattern of Marxists and nationalists were the fascists and other right-wing terrorists that typically appeared in response to the campaigns of Marxist or separatist-nationalist groups (especially where the state was perceived to be 'weak' in confronting the nationalist or Marxist insurgents), and which are consequently thought of as having emerged in 'reverse waves'. See Leonard Weinberg, 'The Fifth Wave?', paper presented at conference on *Current and Future Trends in the Study of Terrorism*, University of Haifa, January 2006; presentation available for viewing at http://video.haifa.ac.il/HTML/HTMLEng/HTMLInner/ Terrorism012006.html.

24 For a detailed overview of the emergence of the Christian Right, see, for example, Allan J. Lichtman, *White Protestant Nation: The Rise of the American Conservative Movement* (New York: Atlantic Monthly Press, 2008), esp. chs 7 and 8.

25 For a fascinating account of how the discourse in the Arab world shifted from secular to religious, see François Burgat, *Face to Face with Political Islam* (London: I. B. Tauris, 2001), ch. 2.

26 Magnus Ranstorp, 'Terrorism in the Name of Religion', reproduced in Russell D. Howard and Reid L. Sawyer (eds), *Terrorism and Counterterrorism: Understanding the New Security Environment* (Guilford, CT: McGraw-Hill, 2003), p. 124.

27 Bruce Hoffman, '"Holy Terror": The Implications of Terrorism Motivated by a Religious Imperative', *Studies in Conflict and Terrorism*, 18(4) (1995): 272. For similar data, albeit based on the US State Department's data, see Brigitte Nacos, *Terrorism and Counterterrorism*, 2nd ed. (New York and London: Penguin, 2008), p. 89.

28 Ekaterina Stepanova, *Terrorism in Asymmetrical Conflict: Ideological and Structural Aspects* (Oxford: Oxford University Press, 2008), p. 57.

29 Ibid., pp. 54–8.

30 On the emergence and evolution of Hamas as a social movement,
    see Shaul Mishal and Avraham Sela, *The Palestinian Hamas:
    Vision, Violence, and Coexistence* (New York: Columbia University
    Press, 2000).
31 See Guido Steinberg, 'Die irakische Aufstandsbewegung: Akteure,
    Strategien, Strukturen', *SWP-Studie*, October 2006: 14–19.
32 Bruce Hoffman, 'The American Perspective', p. 163.
33 Brian Michael Jenkins, 'The Future Course of International
    Terrorism', *The Futurist*, July/August 1987; available at www.wfs.
    org/jenkins.htm.
34 Bruce Hoffman, 'The Emergence of the New Terrorism', in
    Andrew Tan and Kumar Ramakrishna (eds), *The New Terrorism:
    Anatomy, Trends and Counter-Strategies* (Singapore: Eastern
    University Press, 2002), pp. 32, 47.
35 Brian Michael Jenkins, *International Terrorism: A New Kind of
    Warfare* (Santa Monica, CA: RAND, 1974), p. 4.
36 See, for example, Hoffman, 'Terrorism Trends and Prospects', p.
    11; Nacos, *Terrorism and Counterterrorism*, pp. 6–7.
37 Conversation with Gary Ackerman, research director, START
    consortium, University of Maryland, 15 September 2008. Even
    the US National Counterterrorism Center recently conceded
    that, in many cases, it is impossible to differentiate between
    domestic and international terrorism. See Nacos, *Terrorism and
    Counterterrorism*, pp. 8–9.
38 David Tucker, 'What is New about the New Terrorism and How
    Dangerous Is It?' *Terrorism and Political Violence*, 13(3) (2001): 6.
39 The Tokyo nerve gas attack in 1995, for example, may have
    caused only twelve fatalities, but the perpetrators' intention had
    been to kill hundreds, if not thousands.
40 Olivier Roy, 'Radicalisation and De-radicalisation', in
    International Centre for the Study of Radicalisation and Political
    Violence (ICSR), *Perspectives on Radicalisation and Political
    Violence* (London: ICSR, 2008), p. 12.
41 For opposing views on the issue of nuclear terrorism, see – for
    example – Graham Allison, *Nuclear Terrorism: The Ultimate
    Preventable Catastrophe* (New York: Henry Holt, 2004); Robin
    Frost, 'Nuclear Terrorism after 9/11', *Adelphi Paper 378*,
    December 2005.
42 For an excellent overview of attempts by terrorists to use chemical
    and biological weapons, see Tucker, *Toxic Terror*.

43 'IRA Staff Report', cited in Tim Pat Coogan, *The IRA*, 3rd ed. (London: Fontana/Collins, 1987), p. 578.

44 Ibid., p. 579.

45 Ed Moloney, *The Secret History of the IRA* (London: Penguin, 2003), p. 177.

46 Coogan, *The IRA*, p. 579.

47 See Brian Feeney, *Sinn Fein: A Hundred Turbulent Years* (Dublin: O'Brien Press, 2002), ch. 9.

48 Peter R. Neumann, 'The Bullet and the Ballot Box: The Case of the IRA', *The Journal of Strategic Studies*, 28(6) (2005): 959, 964–5.

49 Moloney, *The Secret History*, pp. 461–7.

50 See M. L. R. Smith, *Fighting for Ireland? The Military Strategy of the Irish Republican Movement* (London: Routledge, 1995), p. 124.

51 John McGarry and Brendan O'Leary, *Explaining Northern Ireland* (Oxford: Blackwell, 1995), p. 327. For insights on the broader question of the IRA's international involvement, see Adrian Guelke, *Northern Ireland: The International Perspective* (Dublin: Gill and Macmillan, 1989).

52 J. Bowyer Bell, *IRA: Tactics and Targets* (Dublin: Poolbeg, 1990), p. 9.

53 Republican writer, cited in Smith, *Fighting for Ireland?*, p. 7.

54 Adams, cited in Peter Taylor, *Provos* (London: Bloomsbury, 1997), pp. 283–4.

55 See, for example, Mark Juergensmeyer, *Terror in the Mind of God: The Global Rise of Religious Violence*, 2nd ed. (Los Angeles: University of California Press, 2000), pp. 36–43.

56 Patrick Bishop and Eamonn Mallie, *The Provisional IRA* (London: Corgi, 1987), pp. 149–50.

57 Smith, *Fighting for Ireland?* pp. 23–4.

58 Henry Patterson, *The Politics of Illusion: A Political History of the IRA* (London: Serif, 1997), p. 13.

59 Bishop and Mallie, *The Provisional IRA*, p. 155.

60 Numbers based on Malcolm Sutton's 'Index of Deaths' available on the web site of the Conflict Archive on the Internet (CAIN) at http://cain.ulst.ac.uk/sutton/tables/organisations_responsible.html.

61 Ibid.

62 The Kingsmill attack was carried out by the South Armagh Republican Action Force, 'a flag of convenience for PIRA's units in the border areas of counties Armagh and Tyrone'. See Smith, *Fighting for Ireland?* p. 120.

63 Bishop, *The Provisional IRA*, pp. 258, 337.

64 Bowyer Bell, *IRA*, p. 30.
65 Neumann, 'The Bullet', p. 961.
66 Bowyer Bell, *IRA*, p. 60.
67 Ibid.
68 See, for example, Kevin Toolis, 'Informer: The Life and Death of an IRA Man', *New York Times*, 3 February 1991.
69 For the most authoritative account of Al Qaeda's foundation, see Lawrence Wright, *The Looming Tower: Al-Qaeda's Road to 9/11* (London: Penguin, 2006), esp. ch. 6.
70 This refers to the so-called Bojinka plot in which Ramzi Yousef, who had been behind the first World Trade Center bombing in 1993, was hoping to bring down up to a dozen passenger planes in mid-flight. During a test-run, one passenger on a flight from the Philippines to Tokyo was killed. See Oliver Schröm, *Al Qaida: Akteure, Strukturen, Attentate* (Frankfurt/Main: Links, 2003), ch. 4.
71 'List of Al Qaida inspired terror attacks released', *Prime Minister's Office*, 13 July 2005; available at http://www.number-10.gov.uk/output/Page7930.asp.
72 Cited in Congressional Research Service, 'Terrorist Attacks by Al Qaeda', 31 March 2004. It is worth noting that former President Bill Clinton strongly denies that Black Hawk Down had anything to do with Al Qaeda. In a recent television interview, he claimed that 'no living soul' believed that this was the work of Osama bin Laden and his organization. See 'Transcript: William Jefferson Clinton on "Fox News Sunday"', 26 September 2006; available at http://www.foxnews.com/story/0,2933,215397,00.html.
73 See Paul L. Williams, *Al Qaeda: Brotherhood of Terror* (New York: Alpha, 2002), chs 7 and 8. Also Rohan Gunaratna, *Inside Al Qaeda* (London: Hurst, 2002), esp. ch. 2.
74 See Olivier Roy, 'Netzwerk des Terrors – Markenzeichen al-Qaida', *Le Monde Diplomatique* (German edition), 10 September 2004; Peter Bergen, *Holy War, Inc.: Inside the Secret World of Osama bin Laden* (London: Phoenix, 2001), ch. 10.
75 Bruce Hoffman, 'The Changing Face of Al Qaeda and the Global War on Terrorism', *Studies in Conflict and Terrorism*, 27(6) (2004): 549–60. Also Jessica Stern, 'The Protean Enemy', *Foreign Affairs*, July/August 2003: 354–66.
76 See Jason Burke, *Al Qaeda: The True Story of Radical Islam* (London: I. B. Tauris, 2003).
77 Cited in Brynjar Lia, 'The al-Qaida Strategist Abu Mus'ab

al-Suri: A Profile', OMS-Seminar Presentation, Oslo, 15 March
2006, p. 17; available at http://www.mil.no/multimedia/
archive/00076/_The_Al-Qaida_strate_76568a.pdf.
78 Ibid.
79 Marc Sageman, *Leaderless Jihad: Terror Networks in the Twenty-
First Century* (Philadelphia: University of Pennsylvania Press,
2008), p. 144.
80 Bruce Hoffman, 'The Myth of Grass-Roots Terrorism: Why
Osama bin Laden Still Matters', *Foreign Affairs*, May/June 2008.
81 Ibid.
82 Roy, 'Radicalisation and De-radicalisation', p. 10.
83 The concept of jihad has a variety of meanings in Islamic
theology, but Al Qaeda uses it almost exclusively in the context
of armed struggle. See John Esposito, *Unholy War: Terror in the
Name of Islam* (Oxford: Oxford University Press, 2002), pp. 26–8.
84 Not all Salafis are militant Islamists. For distinctions amongst
followers of the Salafi movement, see Quintan Wiktorowicz,
'Anatomy of the Salafi Movement', *Studies in Conflict and
Terrorism*, 29(3) (2006): 207–39.
85 See Guido Steinberg, *Der nahe und der ferne Feind* (Munich: C.
H. Beck, 2005), chs 1 and 2. For a variety of excellent reports on
Islamist militant ideology issued by the Combating Terrorism
Centre at West Point, see http://ctc.usma.edu/publications/
publications.asp.
86 Jacqui Smith, 'Our Shared Values – A Shared Responsibility',
speech delivered at the *First International Conference on
Radicalisation and Political Violence*, 17 January 2008; available
at http://press.homeoffice.gov.uk/Speeches/sp-hs-terrorism-
keynote-jan-08.
87 Sara Silvestri, 'Radical Islam: Threats and Opportunities', *Global
Dialogue*, 9(3–4) (2007): 119.
88 John Gray, 'The Atheist Delusion', *The Guardian*, 15 March 2008.
89 Olivier Roy, *Globalized Islam: The Search for a New Ummah* (New
York: Columbia University Press, 2004), p. 46.
90 See, for example, 'Full Text: Bin Laden's Letter to America',
The Observer, 24 October 2002; '"The Solution" – A Video
Speech from Usama bin Laden Addressing the American
People on the Occasion of the Sixth Anniversary of 9/11',
SITE Intelligence Institute, September 2007; available at http://
counterterrorismblog.org/site-resources/images/SITE-OBL-

transcript.pdf.

91 30 Jan 2005, Al Zawahiri audiotape.

92 Roy, 'Radicalisation', pp. 11–12.

93 The RAND/MIPT Terrorism Incident Database is maintained by the Oklahoma City National Memorial Institute for the Prevention of Terrorism in collaboration with RAND. See http://www.rand.org/ise/projects/terrorismdatabase/.

94 Peter Bergen and Paul Cruickshank, 'Iraq 101: The Iraq Effect: The War in Iraq and Its Impact on the War on Terrorism', *Mother Jones*, March 2007.

95 See 'List of Al Qaida', *Prime Minister's Office*: Congressional Research Service, 'Terrorist Attacks by Al Qaeda'. The dynamics of the Al Qaeda campaign in Iraq are somewhat different, mainly because Al Qaeda takes part in an insurgency in which it is only one of several players. The overall trend towards mass-casualty attacks against civilian targets, however, holds. Since 2004/05, much of Al Qaeda's attention has been devoted towards attacking Shiite civilian targets, apparently with the intention of triggering a civil war. See Steinberg, 'Die irakische Aufstandsbewegung', pp. 11–13.

96 Ayman Al Zawahiri, 'Why Attack America' (excerpt from *Knights under the Prophet's Banner*), in Barry M. Rubin and Judith C. Rubin (eds), *Anti-American Terrorism and the Middle East* (Oxford: Oxford University Press, 2002), pp. 131–3.

97 For a comprehensive list of Al Qaeda's CBRN activities, see 'Al-Qa'ida's WMD Activities' put together by the Monterey Institute; available at http://cns.miis.edu/pubs/other/sjm_cht.htm.

98 Michael Kenney, *From Pablo to Osama: Trafficking and Terrorist Networks, Government Bureaucracies and Competitive Adaptation* (University Park, PA: Penn State Press, 2007), p. 148.

99 Though it may, of course, at some point decide to carry out attacks against Israelis and/or Jews abroad. See Matthew Levitt, 'Could Hamas Target the West?', *Studies in Conflict and Terrorism*, 30(1) (2007): 925–45.

CHAPTER 3 HOLY WAR, INC.? THE EMERGENCE OF TRANSNATIONAL TERROR NETWORKS

1 Peter L. Bergen, *Holy War, Inc.: Inside the Secret World of Osama bin Laden* (London: Weidenfeld & Nicolson, 2001).

2 Ibid., p. 29.
3 See also Bruce Hoffman, 'The Emergence of the New Terrorism' in Andrew Tan and Kumar Ramakrishna (eds), *The New Terrorism: Anatomy, Trends and Counter-Strategies* (Singapore: Eastern University Press, 2002), pp. 35–6.
4 Jessica T. Matthews, 'Power Shift', *Foreign Affairs*, January/February 1997.
5 Fareed Zakaria, *The Future of Freedom* (New York: W. W. Norton, 2003), p. i.
6 Daniel Byman, *Deadly Connections: States that Sponsor Terrorism* (Cambridge: Cambridge University Press, 2005), p. 2.
7 Zakaria, *The Future of Freedom*, p. i.
8 Walter Laqueur, *The New Terrorism* (Oxford: Oxford University Press, 1999), pp. 13–14.
9 Louis Beam, 'Leaderless Resistance', *The Seditionist*, February 1992. Available at www.louisbeam.com/leaderless.htm.
10 Peter R. Neumann and M. L. R. Smith, *The Strategy of Terrorism* (London: Routledge, 2008), p. 47.
11 See 'A Look Back in TIME: Interview with Timothy McVeigh', *Time Magazine*, 11 May 2001.
12 'A New Age of Satellite Broadcasting Dawns on the Middle East', *Daily Star* (Lebanon), 26 February 2007.
13 See Mohamed Zayani, 'Beacon of Hatred: Inside Hizballah's Al Manar Television', *European Journal of Communication*, 21(2) (2006): 252–6.
14 Anne Marie Baylouny, 'Al Manar and Alhurra: Competing Satellite Stations and Ideologies', *CSRC Discussion Paper 05/49*, September 2005, pp. 4–9.
15 See Manuel Castells, *The Internet Galaxy* (Oxford: Oxford University Press, 2001). Castells's ideas about the information age underlie much of the analysis provided by this and other authors. His most important work of reference is the three-volume *The Information Age* (Oxford: Blackwell 1996–8).
16 Ayman al Zawahiri, quoted in Jarret M. Brachman, 'High-Tech Terror: Al Qaeda's Use of New Technology', *The Fletcher Forum of World Affairs*, 30(2) (2006): 150.
17 See, for example, Daniel Kimmage, 'The Al-Qaeda Media Nexus: The Virtual Network behind the Global Message', *RFE/RL Special Report*, March 2008; Brynjar Lia, 'Al-Qaeda Online: Understanding Jihadist Internet Infrastructure', *Jane's Intelligence*

Review, 1 January 2006.

18 See, for example, Lawrence Wright, 'The Rebellion Within', *The New Yorker,* 2 June 2008.

19 Byman, *Deadly Connections,* p. 2.

20 See, for example, Claire Sterling, *The Terror Network* (New York: Henry Holt, 1981).

21 See Grant Wardlaw, 'Terrorism as an Instrument of Foreign Policy', in David Rapoport (ed.), *Inside Terrorist Organizations,* 2nd ed. (London: Routledge, 2001), pp. 237–59.

22 See Mohammad-Mahmoud Ould Mohamedou, *Understanding Al Qaeda: The Transformation of War* (London: Pluto Press), p. 49.

23 Initially based in Afghanistan, the group relocated to Sudan in the early 1990s, and only returned to Afghanistan when it was threatened with expulsion by the Sudanese government. Following the overthrow of the Taliban regime in late 2001, Al Qaeda then settled across the border in the Tribal Areas of Pakistan. See Bergen, *Holy War, Inc.,* ch. 4; Europol, *European Union Terrorism and Trend Report 2008* (Europol: The Hague, 2008), pp. 21, 24–5.

24 'Letter from al-Zawahiri to al-Zarqawi', released by the Office of the Director of the National Intelligence and reproduced in *Global Security,* 11 October 2005; available at http://www.globalsecurity.org/security/library/report/2005/zawahiri-zarqawi-letter_9jul2005.htm.

25 See Petter Nesser, 'Structures of Jihadist Terrorist Cells in the UK and Europe', paper given at the FFI/King's conference on *The Changing Faces of Jihadism,* London, 28 April 2006. Available at http://www.mil.no/felles/ffi/start/FFI-prosjekter/Alfover/_TERRA/Publikasjoner/Speeches/.

26 National Commission on Terrorist Attacks upon the United States, *The 9/11 Commission Report* (New York: W. W. Norton, 2004), pp. 160–9.

27 Ibid., pp. 168–9.

28 Take, for example, the speed with which information is being processed. In the 1960s, the most advanced data connections were able to transmit information at speeds of 300 bits per second. In 2005, the most basic home computer modems were reaching 60,000 bits per second. See Francis Heylighen, 'Complexity and Information Overload in Society: Why Increasing Efficiency Leads to Decreasing Control', paper

submitted to *The Information Society* (2005); available at http://pespmc1.vub.ac.be/Papers/Info-Overload.pdf.

29 Javier Jordan and Nicola Horsburgh, 'Mapping Jihadist Terrorism in Spain', *Studies in Conflict and Terrorism*, 28(3) (2005): 184. Also Alison Pargeter, *The New Frontiers of Jihad: Radical Islam in Europe* (Philadelphia: University of Pennsylvania Press, 2008), ch. 8.

30 See, for example, Duncan Gardham, 'Osama bin Laden's man in Europe', *Daily Telegraph*, 18 June 2008.

31 Jordan and Horsburgh, 'Mapping Jihadist', p. 176.

32 Ibid., pp. 176–9.

33 Rogelio Alonso, 'Radicalization in Spain', unpublished paper, September 2007.

34 Javier Jordan and Robert Wesley, 'The Madrid Attacks: Results of Investigations Two Years Later', *Jamestown Terrorism Monitor*, 4(5) (2006), http://www.jamestown.org/programs/gta/single/?tx_ttnews%5Btt_news%5D=696&tx_ttnews%5BbackPid%5D=181&no_cache=1

35 Ibid.

36 Jordan and Horsburgh, 'Mapping Jihadist', p. 184.

37 Thomas L. Friedman, *The World Is Flat: A Brief History of the Twenty-First Century* (London: Picador, 2007), ch. 1.

38 See, for example, Daniel Benjamin and Steven Simon, *The Next Attack* (New York: Henry Holt, 2005), pp. 27–31; Aidan Kirby, 'The London Bombers as "Self-Starters": A Case Study in Indigenous Radicalization and the Emergence of Autonomous Cliques', *Studies in Conflict and Terrorism*, 30(5) (2007): 415–28.

39 Friedman coined the idea of 'super-empowered individuals'; see Thomas L. Friedman, *The Lexus and the Olive Tree: Understanding Globalization*, 2nd ed. (New York: Farrar, Straus and Giroux, 2000), p. 13.

40 Marc Sageman, *Leaderless Jihad: Terror Networks in the Twenty-First Century* (Philadelphia: University of Pennsylvania Press, 2008), p. 144.

41 See Lorenzo Vidino, 'The Hofstad Group: The New Face of Terrorist Networks in Europe', *Studies in Conflict and Terrorism*, 30(7) (2007): 579–92; Petter Nesser, 'Jihadism in Western Europe after the Invasion of Iraq: Tracing Motivational Influences from the Iraq War on Jihadist Terrorism in Western Europe', *Studies in Conflict and Terrorism*, 29(4) (2006): 336.

42 Site Institute, 'Irhabi 007 Unveiled: A Portrait of a Cyber-Terrorist',

Site Report, 2006; available at http://www.siteinstitute.org.

43 Yassin Musharbash, '37.000 Kreditkarten für "Terrorist 007"',
Spiegel Online, 26 July 2007; available at http://www.spiegel.de/
politik/ausland/0,1518,495468,00.html.

44 Stefan H. Leader and Peter Probst, 'The Earth Liberation Front
and Environmental Terrorism', *Terrorism and Political Violence,*
15(4) (2003): 37. See also Gary Ackerman, 'Beyond Arson? A
Threat Assessment of the Earth Liberation Front', *Terrorism and
Political Violence,* 15(4) (2003): 143–70.

45 Quoted in Paul Joosse, 'Leaderless Resistance and Ideological
Inclusion: The Case of the Earth Liberation Front', *Terrorism and
Political Violence,* 19 (2007): 352.

46 Quoted in ibid., p. 354.

47 Ibid.

48 For instance, the ELF site makes it very clear that actions taken by
supporters 'are not endorsed, encouraged, or approved of by the
management and participants of this web site'. Quoted in Joosse,
'Leaderless Resistance', p. 354.

49 Ibid., pp. 360–1.

50 Cited in Sidney Tarrow, *The New Transnational Activism*
(Cambridge: Cambridge University Press, 2005), p. 5. According
to a British Council report, one billion people spoke English 'to
one degree or another' in 2004. By 2015, the number is predicted
to rise to three billion. See Tom Still, 'English as the lingua
franca of a new age: It's more powerful than any law', *Wisconsin
Technology Network News,* 29 May 2006.

51 Olivier Roy, *Globalized Islam: The Search for a New Ummah* (New
York: Columbia University Press, 2004), p. 304.

52 British journalist Shiv Malik, interview with author, 10 July 2007.

53 Sageman, *Leaderless Jihad,* p. 110.

54 See, for example, Fred Halliday, 'Global Governance: Problems
and Prospects', *Citizenship Studies,* 4(1) (2000): 19–33.

55 See Leon Brittan, *Globalisation vs. Sovereignty? The European
Response: The 1997 Rede Lecture and Related Speeches and Articles*
(Cambridge: Cambridge University Press, 1998).

56 Tarrow, *The New Transnational Activism,* pp. 64–8.

57 Ibid., p. 64.

58 Ibid., p. 68.

59 See, for example, Greg Buckman, *Globalization: Tame It or Scrap
It?* (London: Zed Books, 2004); Amory Starr, *Naming the Enemy:*

Anti-Corporate Social Movements Confront Globalization (London: Zed Books, 2001).

60 For detailed accounts of the various campaigns, see Gilles Kepel, *Jihad: The Trail of Political Islam* (London: I. B. Tauris, 2003).

61 Abdel Bari Atwan, *The Secret History of Al-Qa'ida* (London: Abacus, 2006), pp. 37–9.

62 Zawahiri, quoted in Guido Steinberg, *Der nahe und der ferne Feind: Die Netzwerke des islamistischen Terrorismus* (Munich: C. H. Beck, 2005), p. 61.

63 Ibid., p. 59.

64 Tarrow, *The New Transnational Activism*, ch. 4.

65 Ibid., pp. 75–6.

66 Ibid.

67 Peter Bergen, *The Osama bin Laden I know: An Oral History of al Qaeda's Leader* (New York: Free Press, 2006), p. 258.

68 See Jean-Luc Marret, 'Al-Qaeda in the Islamic Maghreb: A "Glocal" Organization', *Studies in Conflict and Terrorism*, 31(6) (2008): 543.

69 Jonah Goldstein and Jeremy Rayner, 'The Politics of Identity in Late Modern Society', *Theory and Society*, 23 (1994): 370. Also Anthony Giddens, *Modernity and Self-Identity: Self and Society in the Late Modern Age* (Cambridge: Polity, 1991), p. 54.

70 See, for example, David Held, *Democracy and the Global Order* (Cambridge: Polity, 1995), pp. 232–3.

71 See International Organization for Migration, *World Migration Report 2005* (IOM: Geneva, 2005), Section 3. Available at http://www.iom.int.

72 This 'speculation' is based on data from countries where statistics on 'second generation' migrants are available. For the case of the United States, see Population Reference Bureau, *Population Bulletin*, 62(3) (2007): 8; available at http://www.prb.org/pdf07/62.3Highlights.pdf.

73 For an overview of various debates, see Philip Spencer and Howard Wollman, *Nationalism: A Critical Introduction* (London: Sage, 2002), chs 6 and 7.

74 AIVD, *Recruitment for the Jihad in the Netherlands: From Incident to Trend*, AIVD Briefing Paper, December 2002; available at https://www.aivd.nl/actueel_publicaties/aivd-publicaties/recuirtment_for_the. See also Michael Taarnby, *Recruitment of Islamist Terrorists in Europe: Trends and Perspectives*, research report funded by the Danish Ministry of Justice, January 2005,

pp. 29–37.

75 Marc Sageman, *Understanding Terror Networks* (Philadelphia: Pennsylvania University Press, 2004), ch. 3.

76 Quoted in Peter R. Neumann, 'The Appeal of Jihad', *International Herald Tribune*, 5 July 2007.

77 See Peter R. Neumann, 'Europe's Jihadist Dilemma', *Survival*, 48(2) (2006): 73–4.

78 Olivier Roy, *Globalized Islam: The Search for a New Ummah* (New York: Columbia University Press, 2004), p. 305.

79 Ibid.

80 Ibid., p. 309.

81 Ibid., p. 303.

82 A collation of statistics detailing all these developments is provided by the *Global Policy Forum* and can be found at http://www.globalpolicy.org/globaliz/charts/index.htm.

83 See, for example, Zahera Harb and Ehab Bessaiso, 'British Arab Muslim Audiences and Television after September 11', *Journal of Ethnic and Migration Studies*, 32(6) (2006): 1063–76.

84 Interview with Ibn Khattab, quoted in Cerwyn Moore and Paul Tumelty, 'Foreign Fighters and the Case of Chechnya: A Critical Assessment', *Studies in Conflict and Terrorism*, 31(5) (2008): 417.

85 Ibid.

86 Timothy L. Thomas, 'Al Qaida and the Internet: The Danger of Cyberplanning', *Parameters*, 33(2) (2003): 112–23.

87 See Marc Sageman, *Understanding Terror Networks* (Philadelphia: Pennsylvania University Press), p. 161.

88 'Recruitment and Mobilisation for the Islamist Militant Movement in Europe', study carried out by the *International Centre for the Study of Radicalisation and Political Violence* (ICSR), October 2008; available at http://www.icsr.info.

89 Imam Abu Musa, interviewed August 2007.

90 Bob Lambert, former head of London Metropolitan Police's Muslim Contact Unit, interviewed August 2007.

CHAPTER 4 FROM MARX TO MOHAMMED?
RELIGION AND TERRORISM

1 Bruce Hoffman, *Inside Terrorism*, 2nd ed. (New York: Columbia University Press, 2006), p. 83. Also Peter Waldmann,

Terrorismus: Provokation der Macht, 2nd ed. (Hamburg: Murmann, 2005), pp. 124–8.

2 Ibid., p. 47.

3 Hoffman, *Inside Terrorism*, p. 84.

4 See Margaret C. Jacob, *The Enlightenment: A Brief History with Documents* (London: St Martin's, 2000), ch. 1.

5 John Gray, *Al Qaeda and What It Means to Be Modern* (New York and London: The New Press, 2003), p. 7.

6 See Peter Gay, *The Enlightenment: The Rise of Modern Paganism* (New York: Knopf, 1966), especially Book Two. More recently, scholars have argued that Christianity – far from being the enemy – has been instrumental in giving rise to the Enlightenment, albeit inadvertently. See, for example, S. J. Barnett, *The Enlightenment and Religion: Myths of Modernity* (Manchester: Manchester University Press, 2003).

7 For a selection of writings by key Enlightenment thinkers on the issue of religion and reason, including Voltaire's 'Reflections on Religion', see Isaac Kramnick, *The Portable Enlightenment Reader* (New York: Penguin, 1995), Part Three.

8 For various surveys, see Detlef Pollack, 'Religious Change in Europe: Theoretical Considerations and Empirical Findings', in Gabriel Motzkin and Yochi Fischer (eds), *Religion and Democracy in Contemporary Europe* (London: Alliance Publishing, 2008), pp. 83–100.

9 Gilles Kepel, *The Revenge of God: The Resurgence of Islam, Christianity and Judaism in the Modern World* (University Park, PA: Pennsylvania State University Press, 1994), pp. 6–9.

10 Ibid., p. 3.

11 Ibid., p. 2.

12 Frank J. Lechner, 'Global Fundamentalism' in William H. Swatos (ed.), *A Future for Religion?* (London: Sage, 1993), p. 28.

13 See John Naisbitt, *Global Paradox* (New York: Avon, 1995).

14 Benjamin R. Barber, *Jihad vs. McWorld* (New York: Ballantine, 1995), p. 157.

15 See, for example, ibid., pp. 164–5.

16 George F. Will, 'Building a Wall Against Talent', *Washington Post*, 26 June 2008.

17 Thomas Homer Dixon, *The Upside of Down: Catastrophe, Creativity, and the Renewal of Civilization* (New York: Island Press, 2008), p. 127.

18 See Ulrich Beck, *Weltrisikogesellschaft* (Frankfurt/Main: Suhrkamp, 2007), p. 26.

19 Ulrich Beck, *Risikogesellschaft: Auf dem Weg in eine andere Moderne* (Frankfurt/Main: Suhrkamp, 1986), ch. 2.

20 For example, the UK's Office of National Statistics recently announced that it had recorded the highest divorce rates since records began. In the United States, the number of couples who stay together for more than ten years after getting married dropped from over 90 per cent in the 1950s to less than 50 per cent in the 1990s. See Richard Force, 'Getting Married? It Could End in Divorce', *The Times*, 28 March 2008.

21 John Tomlinson, 'Globalization and Cultural Identity' in David Held and Anthony McGrew, *The Global Transformations Reader: An Introduction to the Globalization Debate*, 2nd ed. (Cambridge: Polity, 2003), pp. 271–2.

22 Ibid., p. 274.

23 See Saskia Sassen, *Globalization and Its Discontents: Essays on the New Mobility of People and Money* (New York: Free Press, 1998), esp. ch. 1. Also Saskia Sassen, *Losing Control? Sovereignty in an Age of Globalization* (New York: Columbia University Press, 1996).

24 Mustapha Kamal Pasha, 'Globalization, Islam and Resistance' in Barry K. Gills (ed.), *Globalization and the Politics of Resistance* (Basingstoke: Palgrave, 2000), p. 250.

25 Ibid.

26 Jamal R. Nassar, *Globalization and Terrorism: The Migration of Dreams and Nightmares* (Oxford: Rowman and Littlefield, 2005), p. 104.

27 Ibid., p. 14.

28 Ted Robert Gurr, 'Economic Factors' in Club de Madrid (ed.), *Addressing the Causes of Terrorism* (Madrid: Club de Madrid, 2005), p. 22; available at www.clubmadrid.org.

29 Anand Giridharadas, 'The Paradox of "Choice" in a Globalized Culture', *International Herald Tribune*, 12 September 2008.

30 Barber, *Jihad vs. McWorld*, pp. 164–5.

31 For various examples of the nationalist revival, especially in the Balkans and the Caucasus, see Jan Koehler and Christoph Zürcher (eds.), *Potentials of Disorder* (Manchester: Manchester University Press, 2003).

32 Herfried Münkler, *Die neuen Kriege* (Hamburg: Rowohlt, 2004), ch. 2.

33 Jerrold M. Post, *The Mind of the Terrorist: The Psychology of Terrorism from the IRA to Al-Qaeda* (Basingstoke: Palgrave, 2007), p. 240.

34 See Lawrence Wright, 'The Rebellion Within', *The New Yorker*, 2 June 2008.

35 This thesis has been advanced by numerous scholars. See, for example, Mark Juergensmeyer, *The New Cold War? Religious Nationalism Confronts the Secular State* (Berkeley and Los Angeles: University of California Press, 1993); Martin E. Marty and R. Scott Appleby (eds), *Fundamentalisms and the State: Remaking Polities, Economies and Militance* (Chicago: University of Chicago Press, 1993).

36 Abdulwahab Al Masseri, quoted in Anouar Majid, *Unveiling Traditions: Postcolonial Islam in a Polycentric World* (Durham, NC: Duke University Press, 2000), p. 118. Also Ghassan Salamé, 'Islam and the West', *Foreign Policy*, Spring 1993.

37 See François Burgat, *Face to Face with Political Islam* (London: I. B. Tauris, 2001), ch. 1.

38 Fundamentalists do not like being called fundamentalist, and there has been a considerable amount of debate about the meaning and correct use of the term, especially in the Muslim context. See, for example, Fred Halliday, *Two Hours that Shook the World: September 11, 2001* (London: Saqi Books, 2002), ch. 2. Also Bernard Lewis, *The Crisis of Islam: Holy War and Unholy Terror* (London: Weidenfeld and Nicolson, 2003), pp. 15, 17–18.

39 John H. Garvey, 'Fundamentalism and Politics', in Marty and Appleby, *Fundamentalisms and the State*, p. 15.

40 Michael W. Apple, 'Away with All Teachers: The Cultural Politics of Homeschooling', in Bruce S. Cooper (ed.), *Home Schooling in Full View: A Reader* (Greenwich, CO: Information Age Publishing, 2005), p. 80.

41 Gilles Kepel, *Jihad: The Trail of Political Islam* (London: I. B. Tauris, 2003), p. 221. See also Alison Pargeter, *The New Frontiers of Jihad: Radical Islam in Europe* (Philadelphia: Pennsylvania University Press, 2008), pp. 9–10.

42 Needless to say, where 'fundamentalists' belonged to a faith that was aiming to make converts, this approach also provided a platform for spreading the faith.

43 Leonard Weinberg, 'Turning to Terror: The Conditions under which Political Parties Turn to Terrorist Activities', *Comparative Politics*, 23(4) (1991).

44 Peter R. Neumann and M. L. R. Smith, *The Strategy of Terrorism: How It Works, and Why It Fails* (London: Routledge, 2008), p. 33.

45 John Horgan refers to the idea of 'catalysts'. See John Horgan, *The Psychology of Terrorism* (London: Routledge, 2005), pp. 87–90.

46 Ibid., p. 43.

47 See Andrew Silke, 'The Role of the Organisation in Suicide Terrorism', *International Journal of Mental Health and Addiction*, 4 (2006); available at http://www.ijma-journal.com/issues.php. I also wish to thank Marc Sageman for helping me to understand the importance of 'moral outrage', which he elaborates on in his most recent book. See Marc Sageman, *Leaderless Jihad: Terror Networks in the Twenty-First Century* (Philadelphia: Pennsylvania University Press, 2008), pp. 72–5.

48 Farhad Khosrokhavar, *Les Nouveaux Martyrs d'Allah* (Paris: Flammarion, 2002), p. 152.

49 Sageman, *Leadlerless Jihad*, p. 73.

50 Jessica Stern, *Terror in the Name of God: Why Religious Militants Kill* (New York: HarperCollins, 2003), p. 159.

51 Mark Juergensmeyer, *Terror in the Mind of God: The Global Rise of Religious Violence* (Berkeley and Los Angeles: University of California Press, 2000), chs 8 and 9.

52 See Hoffman, *Inside Terrorism*, p. 89.

53 For a detailed account of the Army of God's killings, see the web site of the National Abortion Federation; available at http://www.prochoice.org/about_abortion/violence/murders.asp.

54 The document is reproduced, in excerpts, at http://www.skepticfiles.org/misc3/aog-book.htm.

55 Stern, *Terror in the Name of God*, p. 165.

56 Juergensmeyer, *Terror in the Mind of God*, p. 23.

57 Ibid.

58 Ibid., pp. 22–3.

59 See Jennifer Gonnerman, 'The Terrorist Campaign Against Abortion', *Village Voice*, 10 November 1998.

60 This terminology is frequently used on the group's web site. See www.armyofgod.com.

61 Neal Horsley, 'Exploding the Myth of the Army of God', available at http://www.christiangallery.com/ExplodingArmyofGodMyth.htm.

62 See Stern, *Terror in the Name of God*, pp. 147–66.

63 See, for example, Olivier Roy, *Globalized Islam: The Search for a New Ummah* (New York: Columbia University Press, 2004), p. 59.

64 John Esposito, *Unholy War: Terror in the Name of Islam* (Oxford: Oxford University Press, 2002), p. 51.

65 Ibid., p. 56.

66 John Esposito, 'Terrorism and the Rise of Political Islam', in Louise Richardson, *The Roots of Terrorism* (London and New York: Routledge, 2006), p. 149.

67 Ibid. See also Guido Steinberg, *Der nahe und der ferne Feind: Die Netzwerke des islamistischen Terrorismus* (Munich: C. H. Beck, 2005), p. 19.

68 Kepel, *Jihad: The Trail*, p. 52.

69 Ibid., p. 43.

70 Rached Ghannouchi, quoted in Francois Burgat, *Face to Face with Political Islam* (London: I. B. Tauris, 2003), p. 35.

71 Ibid., p. 31.

72 According to Amal Saad-Ghorayeb, without Iran's political, financial and logistical support, its military capability and organizational development, 'it would have taken an additional 50 years for the [Hezbollah] movement to score the same achievements'. See Amal Saad-Ghorayeb, *Hizbu'llah: Politics and Religion* (London: Pluto, 2002), p. 14.

73 Steinberg, *Der nahe und der ferne Feind*, p. 31.

74 Kepel, *Jihad: The Trail*, p. 120.

75 Steinberg, *Der nahe und der ferne Feind*, p. 21.

76 President Jimmy Carter's National Security Advisor, Zbigniew Brzezinski, quoted in Lawrence Wright, *The Looming Tower: Al Qaeda's Road to 9/11* (London: Penguin, 2006), p. 99.

77 Peter Bergen, *Holy War, Inc.: Inside the Secret World of Osama bin Laden* (London: Weidenfeld & Nicolson, 2001), p. 58.

78 They fought alongside 250,000 Afghan mujahidin; see ibid.

79 A more detailed account of this period can be found in Wright's *Looming Tower*, esp. ch. 6.

80 Such as US President George H. W. Bush, who coined the phrase. See ibid., pp. 160–1.

81 Kepel, *Jihad: The Trail*; Olivier Roy, *The Failure of Political Islam* (Cambridge, MA: Harvard University Press, 1998).

82 Neumann and M. L. R. Smith, *The Strategy of Terrorism*, pp. 86–8.

83 Fawaz Gerges, *The Far Enemy: Why Jihad Went Global* (Cambridge: Cambridge University Press, 2005).

84 A detailed description of Ramzi Yousef, the 'mastermind' of the attack in 1993, can be found in Simon Reeve, *The New Jackals:*

Ramzi Yousef, Osama bin Laden and the Future of Terrorism
(London: Andre Deutsch, 1999), especially chs 1–5.
85 See Roy, *Globalized Islam*, p. 60.

CHAPTER 5 DYING TO KILL? THE RISE OF MASS-
CASUALTY TERRORISM

1 See, for example, Robert Pape, *Dying to Win: The Strategic Logic
of Suicide Terrorism* (New York: Random House, 2005); Ami
Pedahzur, *Suicide Terrorism* (Cambridge: Polity, 2005).
2 See Ami Pedahzur (ed.), *Root Causes of Suicide Terrorism* (London:
Routledge, 2006).
3 Mia Bloom, *Dying to Kill: The Allure of Suicide Terrorism* (New
York: Columbia University Press, 2005).
4 See Andrew Silke, 'The Role of Suicide in Politics, Conflict, and
Terrorism', *Terrorism and Political Violence*, 18(1) (2006): 35–46.
5 Peter Hill, 'Kamikaze, 1943–45', in Diego Gambetta (ed.), *Making
Sense of Suicide Terrorism* (Oxford: Oxford University Press,
2005), pp. 1–41.
6 Tim Pat Coogan, *The IRA*, 3rd ed. (London: Fontana Press, 1987),
p. 682.
7 There is disagreement among scholars whether actual suicide
or merely the expectation of death is sufficient for an attack
to be considered a 'suicide mission'. See Martha Crenshaw,
'Explaining Suicide Terrorism: A Review Essay', *Security Studies*,
16(1) (2007): 137.
8 According to the analyst C. J. M. Drake, ideology 'not only . . .
provides the initial dynamic for the terrorists' actions, but . . .
it sets out the moral framework within which they operate'.
See C. J. M Drake, 'The Role of Ideology in Terrorists' Target
Selection', *Terrorism and Political Violence*, 10(2) (1998): 53. Also
C. J. M. Drake, *Terrorists' Target Selection* (Basingstoke: Palgrave
Macmillan, 1998).
9 Ekaterina Stepanova, *Terrorism in Asymmetrical Conflict:
Ideological and Structural Aspects* (Oxford: Oxford University
Press, 2008), p. 57.
10 National Counterterrorism Center, *2007 Report on Terrorism*
(Washington DC: NCTC, 2008); available at http://www.
terrorisminfo.mipt.org/pdf/NCTC-2007-Report-on-Terrorism.pdf.

11 Their continued existence is thanks largely to their trade in narcotics which has made them the world's richest terrorists. See Rafael Pardo, 'Colombia's Two-Front War', *Foreign Affairs*, July/August 2000. Also Rachel Ehrenfeld, *Narco-Terrorism* (New York: Basic Books, 1990), ch. 4.

12 In much of the existing literature, the rise in mass-casualty attacks is blamed exclusively on religion. In reality, the contrast between nationalism and religion may not be as dramatic as suggested. Arguably, what made religion *seem* different to someone like Mark Juergensmeyer, who studied the rise of religiously motivated terrorism in the 1990s, was that he compared the pure, undiluted religious extremism of groups like Aum Shinrikyo to the 'old' nationalist agendas of groups like the Palestinian Liberation Organization (PLO) and the IRA, whose nationalist instincts had been tempered by left-wing ideology. See Mark Juergensmeyer, *Terror in the Mind of God: The Global Rise of Religious Violence* (Berkeley and Los Angeles: University of California Press, 2000), Part 2.

13 Quoted in Bruce Hoffman, *Inside Terrorism*, 2nd ed. (New York: Columbia University Press, 2006), p. 6.

14 See Steve Bruce, *The Edge of the Union: The Ulster Loyalist Political Vision* (Oxford: Oxford University Press), ch. 2.

15 Jim Cusack and Henry McDonald, *The UVF* (Dublin: Poolbeg, 1997), pp. 132–3.

16 See, for example, Peter Taylor, *Loyalists* (London: Bloomsburg, 1999), p. 116.

17 Ibid., p. 91.

18 Coogan, *The IRA*, pp. 689–90, 695.

19 Quoted in Smith, *Fighting for Ireland?* p. 25.

20 Ibid., pp. 24–30.

21 See Steve Bruce, 'Pro-State Terror: Loyalist Paramilitaries in Northern Ireland', *Terrorism and Political Violence*, 4(1) (1992): 67–88.

22 Joseph Ruane and Jennifer Todd, *The Dynamics of Conflict in Northern Ireland: Power, Conflict and Emancipation* (Cambridge: Cambridge University Press, 1996), p. 126.

23 Caroly Gallaher, *After the Peace: Loyalist Paramilitaries in Post-Accord Northern Ireland* (Ithaca, NY: Cornell University Press, 2007), ch. 3.

24 For a concise introduction to the conflict, see Ludger Mees, *Nationalism, Violence and Democracy: The Basque Clash of Identities*

(Basingstoke: Palgrave, 2003).

25 For more detail on the ideological struggles, see Robert P. Clark, *The Basque Insurgents: ETA, 1952–1980* (Madison, WI: University of Wisconsin Press, 1984), esp. ch. 2.

26 Paddy Woodworth, *Dirty War, Clean Hands: ETA, the GAL and Spanish Democracy* (New Haven and London: Yale University Press, 2001), p. 40.

27 See Cynthia Irvin, *Militant Nationalism: Between Movement and Party in Ireland and the Basque Country* (Minneapolis: University of Minnesota Press, 1999), esp. chs 3–4. Also Robert P. Clark, *The Basque Insurgents: ETA, 1952–80* (Madison: University of Wisconsin Press, 1984).

28 A full set of statistics can be found in Antonio Remiro Brotóns and Carlos Espósito, 'Spain', in Yonah Alexander (ed.), *Combating Terrorism: Strategies of Ten Countries* (Ann Arbor: University of Michigan Press, 2002), pp. 174–6, 178–9.

29 Quoted in Giles Tremlet, 'The Clues that Point towards al-Qaida', *The Guardian*, 12 March 2004.

30 Paddy Woodworth, 'Was it Eta, or a Strike by al-Qaeda?', *The Times*, 12 March 2004.

31 Quoted in John Hooper, 'Basque Country's Relief at Eta Denial is Tinged with Scepticism', *The Guardian*, 13 March 2004.

32 Quoted in ibid.

33 See Herfried Münkler, *Die neuen Kriege* (Hamburg: Rowohlt, 2004), ch. 2.

34 'Transcript of Usama Bin Laden Video Tape', 13 December 2001; available at http://www.defenselink.mil/news/Dec2001/d20011213ubl.pdf.

35 Lawrence Wright, 'The Rebellion Within', *The New Yorker*, 2 June 2008.

36 Ibid.

37 Quoted in Reuven Paz, 'Islamic Legitimacy for the London Bombings', *Occasional Paper of the Project for Research of Islamist Movements* (PRISM), 3(4) (2005); available at www.e-prism.org. Also Yassin Musharbash, *Die neue Al-Qaida: Innenansichten eines lernenden Terrornetzweks* (Cologne: Kiwi, 2006), pp. 143–5.

38 Ibid.

39 Ibid.

40 Wright, 'The Rebellion Within'.

41 Ibid.

42 Ibid.
43 See Joby Warrick, 'U.S. Cites Big Gains Against Al-Qaeda', *Washington Post*, 30 May 2008.
44 Thomas Friedman, 'No Mere Terrorist', *New York Times*, 24 March 2002.
45 Brigitte Nacos, *Terrorism and Counterterrorism*, 2nd ed. (London: Penguin, 2008), p. 224. Also Bruce Hoffman, *Inside Terrorism*, 2nd ed. (New York: Columbia University Press, 2006), pp. 174–9.
46 Walter Laqueur, 'Terrorism – A Balance Sheet', in Walter Laqueur (ed.), *The Terrorism Reader* (Philadelphia: Temple University Press, 1978), p. 261.
47 Donald Roberts and Ulla Foehr, 'Trends in Media Use', *The Future of Children Journal*, 18(1) (2008); available at http://www.comminit.com/en/node/270711.
48 Ofcom, *The Communications Market 2008* (London: Ofcom, 2008); available at http://www.ofcom.org.uk/research/cm/cmr08/keypoints/
49 Guy Paquette, 'Violence on Canadian Television Networks', *The Canadian Child and Adolescent Psychiatry Review*, 13(1) (2004): 13–15.
50 'TV violence on the up', *BBC News*, 25 April 2002.
51 See Dennis Lowry, Tarn Ching Josephine Nio and Dennis Leitner, 'Setting the Public Fear Agenda: A Longitudinal Analysis of Network TV Crime Reporting, Public Perceptions of Crime and FBI Crime Statistics', *Journal of Communication*, 53(1) (2006): 61–73.
52 Craig Anderson, Leonard Berkowitz, Edward Donnerstein et al., 'The Influence of Media Violence on Youth', *Psychological Science in the Public Interest*, 4(3) (2003): 96.
53 Ibid.
54 Quoted in Alex Schmid and Janny Graaf, *Violence as Communication: Insurgent Terrorism and the Western News Media* (London: Sage, 1982), p. 11.
55 *Buffalo Times* interview with McVeigh, quoted in Nacos, *Terrorism and Counterterrorism*, p. 227.
56 Ibid.
57 Ibid.
58 Quoted in Steven K. Paulson, 'Newspaper: McVeigh Admitted to Bombing, Wanted "Body Count"', *Associated Press*, 1 March 1997.
59 Nacos, *Terrorism and Counterterrorism*, p. 222.

60 Quoted in Peter R. Neumann and Alexis Delaney, 'The
    Spectacular Rise of the Female Terrorist', *International Herald
    Tribune*, 6 September 2004.
61 Mia Bloom, 'Palestinian Suicide Bombing: Public Support,
    Market Share, and Outbidding', *Political Science Quarterly*, 119(1)
    (2004): 61–88.
62 For opinion poll data of the period, see ibid., p. 70.
63 Pedahzur, *Root Causes of Suicide Terrorism*, p. 63.
64 Bloom, 'Palestinian Suicide', p. 73.
65 Guido Steinberg, 'Die irakische Aufstandsbewegung: Akteure,
    Strategien, Strukturen', *SWP-Studie 27*, October 2006: 17–19.
66 Michael Boyle, 'The Strategic Logic of Sectarian Killing in Iraq';
    paper presented at the annual meeting of the ISA's 49th Annual
    Convention, San Francisco, 26 March 2008.
67 Ibid., pp. 29–30.
68 Bloom provides an impressive list of instances of historical
    contagion, which includes many of the tactics that were used
    by Palestinian and the so-called 'red' terrorists in the 1970s and
    1980s. See Bloom, *Dying to Kill*, ch. 6.
69 Peter Viggo Jakobsen, 'National Interest, Humanitarianism or
    CNN: What Triggers UN Peace Enforcement After the Cold
    War?', *Journal of Peace Research*, 33(2) (1996): 205–15. For a
    critical perspective, see Piers Robinson, *The CNN Effect: The Myth
    of New, Foreign Policy and Intervention* (London and New York:
    Routledge, 2002).
70 See, for example, Virgil Hawkins, 'The Other Side of the CNN
    Factor: The Media and Conflict', *Journalism Studies*, 3(2) (2002):
    225–40.
71 Russell Jenkins and Daniel McGrory, 'How al-Qaeda tried to
    bring Baghdad to Birmingham', *The Times*, 1 February 2007.
72 Quoted in 'Soldier Kidnap Plotter Given Life', *BBC News*, 18
    September 2008.
73 Shiraz Maher, quoted in Raymond Bonner, Jane Perlez and Eric
    Schmitt, 'British Inquiry of Failed Plots Points to Iraq's Qaeda
    group', *International Herald Tribune*, 14 December 2007.
74 The reason the attack did not work was that the Glasgow plotters
    had failed to anticipate that the entrance doors would be blocked
    by bollards, nor did they have access to military-style explosives.
    Marcus Baram, 'Terror Attacks: Amateur Hour of Al Qaeda
    Operation?', *ABC News*, 3 July 2007.

75 Carl Robichaud, 'The Proliferation of Suicide Bombings', *The Century Foundation*, 10 June 2005.

76 Assaf Moghadam, *The Globalization of Martyrdom: Al Qaeda, Salafi Jihad and the Diffusion of Suicide Attacks* (Washington, DC: Johns Hopkins University Press, 2008), p. 160; see also *Suicide Attacks in Afghanistan (2001–2007)*, report published by the United Nations Assistance Mission to Afghanistan (UNAMA), 1 September 2007, p. 42, available at http://www.unama-afg.org/docs/_UN-Docs/UNAMA%20-%20SUICIDE%20ATTACKS%20STUDY%20-%20SEPT%209th%202007.pdf.

77 See ibid., p. 3.

78 See Seth Jones, 'The Rise of Afghanistan's Insurgency', *International Security*, 32(4) (2008): 34–6.

79 Robichaud, 'The Proliferation of Suicide Bombings'.

80 Peter R. Neumann and M. L. R. Smith, *The Strategy of Terrorism: How It Works and Why It Fails* (London: Routledge, 2008), esp. ch. 5.

81 Ibid., pp. 87–8.

CHAPTER 6 CONFRONTING THE NEW TERRORISM

1 See, for example, Isabelle Duyvesteyn, 'How New Is the New Terrorism?', *Studies in Conflict and Terrorism*, 27 (2004): 439–54.

2 See, for example, Ulrich Schneckener, *Transnationaler Terrorismus* (Frankfurt/Main: Suhrkamp, 2006). A recently published critique of the new terrorism picks up on this point, calling it the 'Al Qaeda exception'. See Thomas Mockaitis, *The 'New' Terrorism: Myths and Reality* (Stanford, CA: Stanford Security Press, 2008), ch. 4.

3 For an excellent survey of key ideas and principles, see Ronald Crelinsten, *Counterterrorism* (Cambridge: Polity, 2009).

4 See Ronald V. Clarke and Graeme R. Newman, *Outsmarting the Terrorists* (Westport, CO: Praeger, 2006).

5 Some of these ideas were developed as early as the 1970s. See, for example, Paul Wilkinson, *Terrorism and the Liberal State* (London: Macmillan, 1977).

6 See Marc Sageman, *Understanding Terror Networks* (Philadelphia: Pennsylvania University Press, 2004).

7 I am grateful to Arie Perliger of the University of Haifa for this insight.

8 See John Arquilla and David Ronfeldt, *Networks and Netwars: The Future of Terror, Crime and Militancy* (Santa Monica, CA: Rand, 2001), ch. 10.

9 Confidential conversation with senior officer, London Metropolitan Police, September 2007.

10 Roundtable on Counter-Terrorism, International Peace Institute, New York, 2 May 2008. See also Jeffrey Laurenti, 'The United Nations and Terrorism', in Leonard Weinberg (ed.), *Democratic Responses to Terrorism* (London and New York: Routledge, 2008), pp. 69–90.

11 I am grateful to Nick Fielding for this insight.

12 Johnny Ryan, *Countering Militant Islamist Radicalisation on the Internet: A User Driven Strategy to Recover the Web* (Dublin: Institute of European Affairs, 2007), ch. 2.

13 Unless, of course, one is willing to give up on the principle of free speech altogether and institute stringent controls on all Internet traffic such as China. I am grateful to Tim Stevens of the International Centre for the Study of Radicalization and Political Violence (ICSR) for this insight.

14 For a discussion of the historical roots of cosmopolitanism, see Thomas Mertens, 'Cosmopolitanism and Citizenship – Kant against Habermas', *European Journal of Philosophy*, 4(3) (1996): 328–47.

15 For an overview, see Derek Heater, *World Citizenship and Government – Cosmopolitan Ideas in the History of Western Political Thought* (Basingstoke: Macmillan, 1996). Also Kwame Anthony Appiah, *Cosmopolitanism: Ethics in a World of Strangers* (New York: W. W. Norton, 2006).

16 See Bruce Ackerman, 'Rooted Cosmopolitanism', *Ethics*, 10(3) (1994): 516–35; Kwame Anthony Appiah, *The Ethics of Identity* (Princeton: Princeton University Press, 2005).

17 Natan Sharanksy (with Shira Wolosky Weiss), *Defending Identity: Its Indispensable Role in Protecting Democracy* (New York: Public Affairs, 2008), pp. 71–2.

18 I wish to thank Richard Pfaltzgraff for this idea.

19 See, for example, Max Abrahms, 'Why Terrorism Does Not Work', *International Security*, 31(2) (2006): 42–78.

20 Jack DuVall, 'Civil Resistance and Alternatives to Violent Struggle' in ICSR, *Perspectives on Radicalisation and Political Violence* (London: ICSR, 2008), pp. 31–7; available at http://icsr.info/Papers.

21 See Frantz Fanon, *The Wretched of the Earth* (New York: Grove Weidenfeld, 1963).

22 See Manfred B. Steger, *Globalism* (New York: Rowman and Littlefield, 2002), ch. 4.

23 Roger Cohen, 'German Official Pessimistic About Far-Right Violence', *New York Times,* 26 August 2000.

24 Richard Barrett, 'Seven Years After 9/11: Al Qaeda's Strengths and Vulnerabilities', *ICSR Future Actions* paper, September 2008; available at www.icsr.info.

25 I am grateful to Stephen Tankel for this insight.

26 Walter Laqueur, *The New Terrorism: Fanaticism and the Arms of Mass Destruction* (Oxford: Oxford University Press, 1999), p. 81.

Select Bibliography

Abrahms, Max (2006), 'Why Terrorism Does Not Work', *International Security*, 31(2): 42–78.

Ackerman, Bruce (1994), 'Rooted Cosmopolitanism', *Ethics*, 10(3): 516–35.

Ackerman, Gary (2003), 'Beyond Arson? A Threat Assessment of the Earth Liberation Front', *Terrorism and Political Violence*, 15(4): 142–70.

Allison, Graham (2004), *Nuclear Terrorism: The Ultimate Preventable Catastrophe*. New York: Henry Holt.

Anderson, Craig Leonard Berkowitz, Edward Donnerstein et al. (2003), 'The Influence of Media Violence on Youth', *Psychological Science in the Public Interest*, 4(3): 81–110.

Anthony Appiah, Kwame (2005), *The Ethics of Identity*. Princeton: Princeton University Press.

Arquilla, John and Ronfeldt, David (eds) (1997), *In Athena's Camp: Preparing for Conflict in the Information Age*. Santa Monica, CA: RAND.

Arquilla, John and Ronfeldt, David (1997), 'The Advent of Netwar' in John Arquilla and David Ronfeldt (eds), *In Athena's Camp: Preparing for Conflict in the Information Age*. Santa Monica, CA: RAND.

Arquilla, John and Ronfeldt, David (2001), *Networks and Netwars: The Future of Terror, Crime and Militancy*. Santa Monica, CA: RAND.

Barber, Benjamin R. (1995), *Jihad vs. McWorld*. New York: Ballantine.

Barrett, Richard (2008), 'Seven Years after 9/11: Al Qaeda's Strengths and Vulnerabilities', *ICSR Future Actions* paper (September).

Bauman, Zygmunt (2000), *Liquid Modernity*. Cambridge: Polity.

Beck, Ulrich (1986), *Risikogesellschaft: Auf dem Weg in eine andere Moderne*. Frankfurt/Main: Suhrkamp.

Beck, Ulrich (2007), *Weltrisikogesellschaft: Auf der Suche nach der verlorenen Sicherheit*. Frankfurt/Main: Suhrkamp.

Beck, Ulrich, Giddens, Anthony and Lash, Scott (1994), *Reflexive Modernization: Politics, Tradition and Aesthetics in the Modern Social Order*. Oxford: Blackwell.

Benjamin, Daniel and Simon, Steven (2002), *The Age of Sacred Terror*. New York: Random House.

Benjamin, Daniel and Simon, Steven (2005), *The Next Attack*. New York: Henry Holt.

Bergen, Peter (2001), *Holy War, Inc.: Inside the Secret World of Osama bin Laden*. London: Phoenix.

Bloom, Mia (2004) 'Palestinian Suicide Bombing: Public Support, Market Share, and Outbidding', *Political Science Quarterly*, 119(1): 61–88.

Bobbitt, Philip (2008), *Terror and Consent: The Wars for the Twenty-First Century*. New York: Knopf.

Boyle, Michael (2008), 'The Strategic Logic of Sectarian Killing in Iraq'. Paper presented at the annual meeting of the ISA's 49th Annual Convention, San Francisco (26 March).

Brachman, Jarret M. (2006), 'High-Tech Terror: Al Qaeda's Use of New Technology', *The Fletcher Forum of World Affairs*, 30(2): 149–64.

Burke, Jason (2003), *Al Qaeda: The True Story of Radical Islam*. London: I. B. Tauris.

Byman, Daniel (2005), *Deadly Connections: States that Sponsor Terrorism*. Cambridge: Cambridge University Press.

Castells, Manuel (1996–8), *The Information Age*, Vols I, II, and III. Oxford: Blackwell.

Castells, Manuel (2001), *The Internet Galaxy*. Oxford: Oxford University Press.

Clarke, Ronald V. and Newman, Graeme R. (2006), *Outsmarting the Terrorists*. Westport, CO: Praeger.

Copeland, Thomas (2001), 'Is the "New Terrorism" Really New? An Analysis of the New Paradigm for Terrorism', *The Journal of Conflict Studies*, 21(2): 91–105.

Crelinsten, Ronald (2009), *Counterterrorism*. Cambridge: Polity.

Crenshaw, Martha (1995) 'Thoughts on Relating Terrorism to

Historical Contexts', in Martha Crenshaw (ed.), *Terrorism in Context*, University Park, PA: Pennsylvania State Press.

Crenshaw, Martha (2007) 'Explaining Suicide Terrorism: A Review Essay', *Security Studies*, 16(1): 133–62.

Drake, C. J. M. (1998) 'The Role of Ideology in Terrorists' Target Selection', *Terrorism and Political Violence*, 10(2): 53–85.

Duyvesteyn, Isabelle (2004) 'How New is the New Terrorism?', *Studies in Conflict and Terrorism*, 27(5): 439–54.

Friedman, Thomas L. (1999), *The Lexus and the Olive Tree*. New York: Farrar, Straus and Giroux.

Friedman, Thomas L. (2007), *The World is Flat: A Brief History of the Twenty-First Century*. London: Picador.

Frost, Robin (2005), 'Nuclear Terrorism after 9/11', Adelphi Paper 378 (December).

Gerges, Fawaz (2005), *The Far Enemy: Why Jihad Went Global*. Cambridge: Cambridge University Press.

Giddens, Anthony (1990), *The Consequences of Modernity*. Cambridge: Polity.

Giddens, Anthony (1991), *Modernity and Self-Identity: Self and Society in the Late Modern Age*. Cambridge: Polity.

Goldstein, Jonah and Rayner, Jeremy (1994), 'The Politics of Identity in Late Modern Society', *Theory and Society*, 23(3): 367–84.

Gray, John (2003), *Al Qaeda and What It Means to Be Modern*. New York and London: The New Press.

Halliday, Fred (2002), *Two Hours that Shook the World: September 11, 2001*. London: Saqi Books.

Heisbourg, Francois (2001), *Hyperterrorisme: la nouvelle guerre*. Paris: Odile Jacob.

Held, David and McGrew, Anthony (2003), *The Global Transformations Reader: An Introduction to the Globalization Debate*, 2nd ed. Cambridge: Polity.

Hirst, Paul and Thompson, Graham (1999), *Globalization in Question*. Cambridge: Polity.

Hoffman, Bruce (1995), '"Holy Terror": The Implications of Terrorism Motivated by a Religious Imperative', *Studies in Conflict and Terrorism*, 18(4): 271–84.

Hoffman, Bruce (2002), 'The Emergence of the New Terrorism', in Andrew Tan and Kumar Ramakrishna (eds), *The New Terrorism: Anatomy, Trends and Counter-Strategies*, Singapore: Eastern University Press.

Hoffman, Bruce (2004) 'The Changing Face of Al Qaeda and the Global War on Terrorism', *Studies in Conflict and Terrorism*, 27(6): 549–60.

Hoffman, Bruce (2006), *Inside Terrorism*, 2nd ed. New York: Columbia University Press.

Hoffman, Bruce (2008), 'The Myth of Grass-Roots Terrorism: Why Osama bin Laden Still Matters', *Foreign Affairs* (May/June): 133–8.

Homer-Dixon, Thomas (2008), *The Upside of Down: Catastrophe, Creativity, and the Renewal of Civilization*. New York: Island Press.

Jacob, Margaret C. (2000), *The Enlightenment: A Brief History with Documents*. London: St Martin's.

Jenkins, Brian M. (1974), *International Terrorism: A New Kind of Warfare*. Santa Monica, CA: RAND.

Jenkins, Brian M. (1987), 'The Future Course of International Terrorism', *The Futurist* (July/August): 8–13.

Jenkins, Brian M. (2001), 'Terrorism and Beyond: A 21st Century Perspective', *Studies in Conflict and Terrorism*, 24(5): 321–7.

Jenkins, Brian M. (2008), *Will Terrorists Go Nuclear?* New York: Prometheus.

Jones, David M. (ed.) (2004), *Globalisation and the New Terror: The Asia Pacific Dimension*. Cheltenham: Edward Elgar.

Joosse, Paul (2007), 'Leaderless Resistance and Ideological Inclusion: The Case of the Earth Liberation Front', *Terrorism and Political Violence*, 19(3): 351–68.

Juergensmeyer, Mark (1993), *The New Cold War? Religious Nationalism Confronts the Secular State*. Berkeley and Los Angeles: University of California Press.

Juergensmeyer, Mark (2000), *Terror in the Mind of God: The Global Rise of Religious Violence*, 2nd ed. Los Angeles: University of California Press.

Kaldor, Mary (1999), *New and Old Wars: Organized Violence in a Global Era*. Stanford: Stanford University Press.

Kaplan, David E. (2000), 'Aum Shinrikyo', in Jonathan B. Tucker (ed.), *Toxic Terror: Assessing Terrorist Use of Chemical and Biological Weapons*, Cambridge, MA: MIT Press.

Kenney, Michael (2007), *From Pablo to Osama: Trafficking and Terrorist Networks, Government Bureaucracies and Competitive Adaptation*. University Park, PA: Penn State Press.

Kepel, Gilles (1994), *The Revenge of God: The Resurgence of Islam,*

Christianity and Judaism in the Modern World. University Park, PA: Pennsylvania State University Press.

Khosrokhavar, Farhad (2002), *Les Nouveaux Martyrs d'Allah.* Paris: Flammarion.

Kirby, Aiden (2007), 'The London Bombers as "Self-Starters": A Case Study in Indigenous Radicalization and the Emergence of Autonomous Cliques', *Studies in Conflict and Terrorism,* 30(5): 415–28.

Laqueur, Walter (ed.) (1978), *The Terrorism Reader.* Philadelphia: Temple University Press.

Laqueur, Walter (1996), 'Postmodern Terrorism: New Rules for an Old Game', *Foreign Affairs,* 75(5): 24–36.

Laqueur, Walter (1999), *The New Terrorism: Fanaticism and the Arms of Mass Destruction.* Oxford: Oxford University Press.

Leader, Stefan H. and Probst, Peter (2003), 'The Earth Liberation Front and Environmental Terrorism', *Terrorism and Political Violence,* 15(4): 37–58.

Lesser, Ian O., Hoffman, Bruce, Arquilla, John, Ronfeldt, David, Zanini, Michele, Jenkins, Brian Michael (eds) (1999), *Countering the New Terrorism.* Santa Monica: RAND.

Marty, Martin E. and Appleby, R. Scott (eds) (1993), *Fundamentalisms and the State: Remaking Polities, Economies and Militance.* Chicago: University of Chicago Press.

Matthews, Jessica T. (1997), 'Power Shift', *Foreign Affairs* (January/ February): 50–66.

Mockaitis, Thomas (2008), *The 'New' Terrorism: Myths and Reality.* Stanford, CA: Stanford Security Press.

Moghadam, Assaf (2008), *The Globalization of Martyrdom: Al Qaeda, Salafi Jihad and the Diffusion of Suicide Attacks.* Washington, DC: Johns Hopkins University Press.

Motzkin, Gabriel and Fischer, Yochi (eds) (2008), *Religion and Democracy in Contemporary Europe.* London: Alliance Publishing.

Münkler, Herfried (2004), *Die neuen Kriege.* Hamburg: Rowohlt.

Musharbash, Yassin (2006), *Die neue Al-Qaida: Innenansichten eines lernenden Terrornetzweks.* Cologne: Kiwi.

Nacos, Brigitte (2008), *Terrorism and Counterterrorism,* 2nd ed. New York and London: Penguin.

Nassar, Jamal R. (2005), *Globalization and Terrorism: The Migration of Dreams and Nightmares.* Oxford: Rowman and Littlefield.

National Commission on Terrorist Attacks upon the United States,

The (2004) *9/11 Commission Report*. New York: W. W. Norton.

Neumann, Peter and Smith, M. L. R. (2008), *The Strategy of Terrorism*. London: Routledge.

Newman, Edward (2004), 'The "New Wars" Debate: A Historical Perspective is Needed', *Security Dialogue*, 35(2): 173–89.

Pargeter, Alison (2008), *The New Frontiers of Jihad: Radical Islam in Europe*. Philadelphia: University of Pennsylvania Press.

'Perspectives on Radicalisation and Political Violence', Papers from the *First International Conference on Radicalisation and Political Violence, ICSR*, London, 17–18 January 2008.

Post, Jerrold M. (2007), *The Mind of the Terrorist: The Psychology of Terrorism from the IRA to Al-Qaeda*. Basingstoke: Palgrave.

Rapoport, David (ed.) (2001), *Inside Terrorist Organizations*, 2nd ed. London: Frank Cass.

Rapoport, David (2002), 'The Four Waves of Rebel Terror and September 11', *Anthropoetics*, 8(1).

Reeve, Simon (1999), *The New Jackals: Ramzi Yousef, Osama bin Laden and the Future of Terrorism*. London: Andre Deutsch.

Richardson, Louise (2006), *The Roots of Terrorism*. London and New York: Routledge.

Robinson, Piers (2002), *The CNN Effect: The Myth of New, Foreign Policy and Intervention*. London and New York: Routledge.

Roy, Olivier (2004), *Globalized Islam: The Search for a New Ummah*. New York: Columbia University Press.

Roy, Olivier, Hoffman, Bruce and Raz, Reuven (2000), 'America and the New Terrorism: An Exchange', *Survival*, 42(2): 156–72.

Sageman, Marc (2004), *Understanding Terror Networks*. Philadelphia, PA: University of Pennsylvania Press.

Sageman, Marc (2008), *Leaderless Jihad: Terror Networks in the Twenty-First Century*. Philadelphia: University of Pennsylvania Press.

Sassen, Saskia (1998), *Globalization and Its Discontents: Essays on the New Mobility of People and Money*. New York: Free Press.

Schmid, Alex and Graaf, Janny (1982), *Violence as Communication: Insurgent Terrorism and the Western News Media*. London: Sage.

Schneckener, Ulrich (2006), *Transnationaler Terrorismus*. Frankfurt/Main: Suhrkamp.

Schulte, Paul (2004), 'Uncertain Diagnosis: Megalomaniacal Hyper-Terrorism and an Unending War for the Future', in David Martin Jones (ed.), *Globalisation and the New Terror: The Asia Pacific*

Dimension, Cheltenham: Edward Elgar.

Sharanksy, Natan (with Shira Wolosky Weiss) (2008), *Defending Identity: Its Indispensable Role in Protecting Democracy*. New York: Public Affairs.

Simon, Steven and Benjamin, Daniel (2000), 'America and the New Terrorism', *Survival*, 42(1): 59–75.

Spencer, Alexander (2006), 'Questioning the Concept of "New Terrorism"', *Peace, Conflict and Development*, 8(8).

Spencer, Philip and Wollman, Howard (2002), *Nationalism: A Critical Introduction*. London: Sage.

Sprinzak, Ehud (1998), 'The Great Superterrorism Scare', *Foreign Policy* (Autumn): 110–24.

Steger, Manfred B. (2002), *Globalism*. New York: Rowman and Littlefield.

Stepanova, Ekaterina (2008), *Terrorism in Asymmetrical Conflict: Ideological and Structural Aspects*. Oxford: Oxford University Press.

Sterling, Claire (1981), *The Terror Network*. New York: Henry Holt.

Stern, Jessica (2003), *Terror in the Name of God: Why Religious Militants Kill*. New York: HarperCollins.

Stern, Jessica (2003) 'The Protean Enemy', *Foreign Affairs* (July/August): 27–40.

Tan, Andrew and Ramakrishna, Kumar (eds) (2002), *The New Terrorism: Anatomy, Trends and Counter-Strategies*. Singapore: Eastern University Press.

Tarrow, Sidney (2005), *The New Transnational Activism*. Cambridge: Cambridge University Press.

Tucker, David (2001), 'What is New about the New Terrorism and How Dangerous Is It?' *Terrorism and Political Violence*, 13(3): 1–14.

Tucker, Jonathan B. (ed.) (2000), *Toxic Terror: Assessing Terrorist Use of Chemical and Biological Weapons*. Cambridge, MA: MIT Press.

Wilkinson, Paul (1977), *Terrorism and the Liberal State*. London: Macmillan.

Wright, Lawrence (2008), 'The Rebellion Within', *The New Yorker*, 2 June.

Zakaria, Fareed (2003), *The Future of Freedom*. New York: W. W. Norton.

Index

Note: page numbers in italics denote figures or tables